Philosophers in Perspective

Kant: The Philosophy of Right

Philosophers in Perspective
General Editor: A. D. Woozley

A series of books designed to throw light on the scope and articulation of the work of the most important philosophers

Published titles
Kant: The Philosophy of Right: Jeffrie G. Murphy
John Stuart Mill: H. J. McCloskey

Forthcoming titles:
Aristotle: J. L. Ackrill
Hegel: H. B. Acton
Berkeley: H. M. Bracken
The French Enlightenment: J. H. Brumfitt
Descartes: Alan Gewirth
Jean-Jacques Rousseau: J. C. Hall
Karl Marx: Eugene Kamenka
Spinoza: Douglas Lewis
Jeremy Bentham: David Lyons
John Locke: J. D. Mabbott
David Hume: T. Penelhum
Plato: Colin Strang

KANT: THE PHILOSOPHY OF RIGHT

Jeffrie G. Murphy

Associate Professor of Philosophy
University of Arizona

Macmillan

St Martin's Press

© Jeffrie G. Murphy 1970

First published 1970 by
MACMILLAN AND CO LTD
London and Basingstoke
Associated companies in New York Toronto
Dublin Melbourne Johannesburg and Madras

Library of Congress catalog card no. 75–108406
SBN (boards) 333 07460 2
(paper) 333 11140 0

Printed in Great Britain by
RICHARD CLAY (THE CHAUCER PRESS), LTD
Bungay, Suffolk

To Lewis White Beck

Acknowledgements

Permission has been given to quote extensive passages from the following translations of works by Kant: *Foundations of the Metaphysics of Morals,* translated by Lewis White Beck, copyright © 1959, by The Liberal Arts Press, reprinted by permission of the Liberal Arts Division of The Bobbs-Merrill Company, Inc. *The Metaphysical Elements of Justice,* translated by John Ladd, copyright © 1965, by the Bobbs-Merrill Company, Inc., reprinted by permission of the College Division of The Bobbs-Merrill Company, Inc. It should be noted that the author has made stylistic changes in these and other translations used and that these changes should not be attributed to the translations. For detailed study of the passages discussed, the reader should consult the translations themselves or Kant's original German.

Contents

Preface

The present study is an attempt to present a critical exposition of Kant's philosophy of right. By a 'philosophy of right' I understand an attempt to discover those principles definitive of the moral rectitude of *actions*. The contrast here is with a theory of virtue – an attempt to characterise (generally in terms of motives) the morally worthy *agent*. The large place in the literature on Kant's ethics has stressed his conception of virtue, where discussions of such mentalistic notions as 'respect for duty' and 'the good will' abound. By focusing upon the philosophy of right, I do not intend to depreciate Kant's theory of virtue. Rather, in keeping with the thrust of this series, I focus upon the philosophy of right because it is here that principles are presented which illuminate the issues of social and political ethics – viz. duties to others which are *prima facie* a proper object of enforcement through State coercion. There is some controversy over whether or not Kant regards *pflichtmässig* or right actions as capable of having any moral worth at all; however, since I have discussed this question in detail elsewhere,[1] I shall here simply assume that *pflichtmässig* actions (i.e. externally right actions considered without regard to the motive which prompts them) are a proper object of moral evalution and can be said to have moral worth.

Parts of an earlier draft of this manuscript were read by Professors Robert L. Holmes and Lewis White Beck of the University of Rochester, and by Professor Gareth Matthews, my former colleague at the University of Minnesota. I have learned much from their helpful comments but have, no doubt to my eventual regret, resisted their enlightenment at many points. And so the usual claim for sole responsibility for error is quite

9

in order. Professor Holmes is owed a special debt of thanks. He advised my doctoral dissertation, from which part of the present study is drawn, and clarified my thought at many crucial points. To Professor Beck I owe my original interest in Kant and most of what I know of the Kantian philosophy. His courses and seminars were the high point of my graduate study. And so, in spite of its weaknesses and the extent to which I am sure he would disagree with much of it, the present study is dedicated to him.

I should also like to thank Professor A. D. Woozley, the general editor of this series, for his careful and illuminating comments on an earlier draft of the entire manuscript. What now confronts the reader is shorter, more intelligible and more free of error than it would have been without his scrutiny.

The Graduate School of the University of Minnesota provided me with a grant, for which I am very grateful, to aid in the completion of the manuscript.

Finally, I should like to express gratitude to my parents and apologies to my wife. My parents were a constant source of assistance and encouragement throughout all of my university studies. And my wife has learned the hard way that the writing of philosophy is not inclined to produce in the writer that kind of temperament and composure generally called philosophical.

In making the always difficult choice between a cumbersome text and numerous notes, I have (for better or worse) adopted the latter alternative. Since many of these notes expand or qualify the argument of the text in important ways, I hope that the reader will not choose to ignore them entirely.

JEFFRIE G. MURPHY

A Note on the Texts

Unless otherwise noted, all references to Kant's works are to the edition issued by the Royal Prussian Academy in Berlin. The volumes of the Academy edition which contain the principal works cited are as follows:

In quoting from these works, I have placed the page number from the Academy edition immediately following the title citation. This is followed by the page numbers of the translation on which I have relied (with occasional modifications) and the name of the translator. For example, a citation from the *Founda-*

tions of the Metaphysics of Morals would appear as follows:

(*Foundations*, 398; Beck, 14)

There are three exceptions to this general procedure. In quoting from the *Critique of Pure Reason*, I follow the standard practice of citing the page numbers from both the 1781 first ('A') and 1787 second ('B') editions of that work. For example:

(*Critique of Pure Reason*,
A 841 = B 869; Kemp Smith, 659)

Also, in quoting from the pre-critical *Lectures on Ethics*, I have relied exclusively on the English translation by Louis Infield and all page references are to this translation. In using Kant's 1770 *Inaugural Dissertation* (*Form and Principles of the Sensible and Intelligible World*) I have relied on the English translation (from the Latin) by John Handyside.

Full publication particulars for all these works may be found in the Bibliography.

1 Kant's Life and Thought

Intellectual Biography; The Pre-critical Philosophy

Biography of Kant is of necessity intellectual biography. For his personal life was, even for a philosopher, remarkably uneventful. As an abundance of
caricatures and anecdotes testify, the most interesting
thing about Kant's personal life was its apparently
thoroughgoing dullness. Born in Königsberg (now
Kaliningrad) in 1724, the son of a saddler, Kant's early
life was influenced by the deep religious atmosphere of
his home. His parents were Pietists, part of a German
Protestant movement which stressed the religious importance of personal integrity and purity of soul over
worldly accomplishments. Kant's own characteristic
devotion to the ideals of duty and moral earnestness
no doubt grew out of this home environment. From
1732 to 1740 he prepared for the university at the Col-
legium Fredericianum, and from 1740 to 1746 studied
physics, mathematics, philosophy and theology at the
University of Königsberg. Königsberg was by no means
the most distinguished of the German universities, but
Kant found sufficient contentment there to make this
university his academic home for the remainder of his
life. After a period of private tutoring, during which
he refused an offer from the University of Jena, Kant
received his doctorate in 1755 and became a *Privat-
dozent* (special lecturer) at Königsberg. He also served
for a time as assistant librarian at the Royal Library.
From 1770 to 1797 he was Professor of Logic and
Metaphysics at Königsberg. He never married and
lived his entire life in this small Prussian city and its
vicinity. He died in 1804.

Much more exciting than Kant's personal life, of
course, is the development of his thinking on the

major problems of philosophy. He contributed master-ful works on epistemology, metaphysics, ethics, politi-cal philosophy and aesthetics. His first major work, however, the *Critique of Pure Reason*, did not appear until he was fifty-seven years old. This, though obvi-ously a work of great genius, was not a work of out-standing brilliance or immediate insight. Rather it was the painstaking result of years of reflection and re-examination of certain recurring puzzles in epistemo-logy and metaphysics that occupied Kant's thought throughout his entire life. Thus a brief examination of Kant's early writings will be useful to place his most famous work in an understandable perspective. Kant is always best understood, at least initially, in terms of what he is reacting against. This reaction, though primarily against leading tenets of empiricism and rationalism, is also often a reaction against his own previous thought.

Kant's early writings are generally referred to as *pre-critical*. This has a philosophical as well as a chrono-logical significance. Chronologically, the pre-critical writings are simply those which antedate the publica-tion of the three great *Critiques*: the *Critique of Pure Reason* (1781), the *Critique of Practical Reason* (1788) and the *Critique of Judgment* (1790). Philosophically, however, the distinction between Kant's pre-critical and critical periods is much more significant. Kant's critical philosophical period begins prior to the actual publication of the first *Critique*, when Kant abandoned his early work as a traditional rationalist (or, as he later says, 'dogmatic') metaphysician and developed his own unique and characteristic philosophical method. This method, the *transcendental* method, matured in reaction against parts of his own earlier *Inaugural Dissertation* and not, as the standard his-torical cliché has it, solely in reaction against Hume. His reading of Hume did not really awaken him from 'dogmatic slumbers' at all. It merely provided extra stimulus for an awakening that had already taken place prior to 1772 when Kant, as revealed in a famous letter to Marcus Herz, developed serious worries about his own metaphysical views as they had found expression in the *Dissertation*. The impact of Hume upon Kant is of undoubted importance, but it is simplistic to claim that Kant, in the absence of reading Hume, would never have developed the mature critical philosophy. This is simplistic, first, because it is evident that Kant had worries of his own about the arguments of the *Dissertation*, and second, because it is easy to overestimate the weaknesses of the *Dissertation* itself. For the *Dissertation*, though parts are open to serious objection, still contains much that is recognisably Kantian and critical in the philosophical sense. Thus it will be illuminating to consider the teachings of the *Dissertation* and Kant's later reasons for unhappiness with some of them. We shall then be in a better position to evaluate the precise character of Hume's impact.[1]

Kant's 1770 *Inaugural Dissertation: Form and Principles of the Sensible and Intelligible World* develops in response to a typically Kantian worry: How is the experience that we do have actually possible? What does one have to presuppose in order to account for knowledge that we do have? The raising of this particular kind of question, the search for presuppositions, is what Kant later calls a *transcendental* inquiry. And the raising of such questions is perhaps the most characteristic mark of the Kantian philosophy. Kant, in critically examining the work of any philosopher, is constantly concerned to raise the question: Are the philosophical claims made by this philosopher compatible with the knowledge and experience that we do have? If not, then we must replace these claims with others which will both (i) be compatible with this experience and knowledge and (ii) account for the nature and possibility of this experience and knowledge. The philosophy under examination in the *Dissertation* is the metaphysics of Leibniz and his follower Christian Wolff.

Kant's initial worry, as he phrases it in the *Dissertation*, is to provide an explication of the concept of a *world*. A world is an intelligible order among things and events. We have a common-sense world of experience, and natural science claims to study the world.

And Kant's question is whether or not a multiple of Leibnizian monads could form a world in the sense that there is a scientific or common-sense world. Kant is constantly impressed by the undeniable fact that our world is not a 'blooming buzzing confusion' but is ordered and intelligible. It can be described and understood both in common sense and science, and Kant will have no truck with any philosophical position which would undermine such a world. Like G. E. Moore in our own day, Kant is persuaded that our common-sense and scientific knowledge is far more certain than is any philosophical premise that someone might employ to make us doubt our possession of this knowledge. The Leibnizian claim that much of our common-sense world is illusion is an immediate sign that there is something wrong somewhere within this particular rationalistic position.

On Leibniz's view, the world is formed of mathematical points (monads) that are *incapable of interacting*. Every monad is a subject, and all predicates true of it are *analytically* true of it. Otherwise it would be a different monad. Thus all connections between a subject and its predicates are logically necessary. Interaction between monads would be contingent connection, and thus there is no interaction. What seems to us (in illusion) to be contingent interaction, causal connection, is seen by God to be merely analytic unpacking of the subject term in question. That Caesar crossed the Rubicon is a logical truth about Caesar and not, as it appears, merely a contingent claim that might have been otherwise. Kant first attacked this view in his *Thoughts on the True Estimation of Living Forces* (1747) and continues the attack in the *Dissertation*.

The general strategy of Kant's attack on Leibniz is to show that there is a necessary condition for the application of the concept of a world, and that an acceptance of the Leibnizian position would render satisfaction of this condition impossible. For a world is possible to describe only if we employ the concept of *wholeness*. Wholeness is an absolute totality of all parts. It is not merely an aggregate of all parts but also

16

manifests systematic interconnection between these parts. If there were not systematic interconnection, then these parts could not form part of my conscious-ness and would, as Kant later says in the first *Critique*, be 'as nothing to me'.

Kant's general argument against Leibniz, then, is simply that there must be interactions between sub-stances or else they would not form one world, would fail to satisfy the condition of wholeness. There would be as many worlds as there are substances. On Leib-niz's view we have an aggregate of substances. But the worlds of science and common sense are not mere aggregates; they are worlds of systematic interconnec-tions. Thus, however interesting Leibniz's theory is in its own right, it cannot present an adequate account of those conditions which explain the possibility of the experience of common sense and the knowledge of science. Indeed, it is ultimately incompatible with such experience and knowledge.

Kant's own alternative to the Leibnizian model is to claim that what form substances into a world are just *principles for the possible interaction of these sub-stances*. And thus the real enterprise of metaphysics should be the discovery of these principles. A plurality of substances form an intelligible world only because they can be described coherently in terms of certain basic principles. In the first *Critique*, Kant will call such principles the *categories*. A category, like that of causation (every event has a cause), is a principle which must be presupposed in order intelligibly to describe a world. It is a condition of conceptual *pos-sibility* and not, as is a law of science, merely a descrip-tion of actuality. Categories order the world, not (as Kant's psychological idiom might suggest) by acting like a sausage machine in forming objects out of the random meat of sensation, but conceptually or lin-guistically. They are not psychological faculties. Rather they are basic *rules* which must be presupposed in order to give sense to any language we might use in describ-ing a world (or, if you prefer, the concepts we use in thinking a world).[2] Indeed, the position (particularly in the *Dissertation*) is really a kind of idealism: the nature of the world is limited by what it makes sense to say. Thus to discover the rules which are presupposed by our discourse about the world and give that discourse meaning is also to discover something about the world. Wittgenstein's famous claims in the *Tractatus* that language limits the world are Kantian in spirit.[3]

Kant then is concerned to argue that certain rules or principles describing possible interactions among substances must be presupposed if we are to have a world like the one we do have – that is, one which is susceptible of coherent description. But why, Kant now asks, have philosophers been tempted to doubt the existence of such principles? He feels that an examination of this question may reveal something important about the enterprise of metaphysics itself and the status of its claims about the world.

Kant poses the question in terms of an antinomy. An antinomy is produced when a thesis and its denial (its antithesis) are both seemingly provable by indisputable arguments. Kant has argued that we *must* employ the concept of wholeness in order to account for our ordered world. But he feels that there is an equally powerful argument to prove that we *cannot* employ such a concept. Thus we are presented with an antinomy.

Now the argument to support the claim that we cannot employ the concept of wholeness has two premises: (1) 'The unrepresentable and the impossible are equivalent in meaning. Anything we cannot imagine is impossible.' (2) 'We cannot imagine the totality of all substances because, since they are infinite, we simply do not have enough time. We cannot hold them all together in imagination.'

Kant is generally prepared to accept this argument. But since he has already defended the claim that we must employ the concept that the argument establishes the impossibility of employing, he appears in serious trouble. His way out is to argue that both the thesis (we must employ the concept of wholeness) and the antithesis (we cannot employ this concept) are true, but true of *different worlds*. We must, he argues,

18

distinguish between things known through Sensibility and things known through Intellect, between the sensible world and the intellectual world. Each world is defined in terms of its organising principles. Kant argues that our sensible or empirical knowledge is limited by representation or imagination. For what is empirically possible is limited to that which can be imagined or, to use his technical term, is presentable to *intuition*. But certain principles, like the wholeness of our world, are obviously knowable, since we know that without them our world would not have the ordered form it manifests. However, because these principles are not representable, they are not knowable sensibly or empirically. Thus they must be knowable to Reason or Intellect, which is not limited (as is Sensibility) by the principle that what is knowable is confined to what is representable. Metaphysical knowledge is thus discovered by Reason and, being knowledge of the intellectual rather than the sensible world, is not subject to a limitation by imagination. Thus the totality of our knowledge demands both Sensibility and Intellect. Here is the beginning of Kant's famous synthesis of empiricism and rationalism.

What is striking about Kant's argument in the *Dissertation* is that he envisions it as an attempt to *save* rationalistic metaphysics. That is, he thinks that the normal objections to rational metaphysical claims arise when one forgets that Reason's competence is not limited by the sort of conditions which limit sensible knowledge. To confuse the limiting principles appropriate to each world is to be guilty of the fallacy of *subreption*, the illegitimate extension of one faculty into the domain of the other. Sensibility is here the enemy, for it attempts to place an unjustified limitation on the Intellect. And the general character of the fallacy is the following: In any judgment 'S is P', the predicate seems to be universally asserted of the subject. But (and this is crucial) if P is a sense predicate it will not be strictly universal of S, but only universal of S in so far as we are spelling out the possibility of S's being known sensibly. The fallacy might arise, for example, in confusing the following two claims: (1)

'Whatever is somewhere exists' and (2) 'Whatever exists is somewhere'.

The latter claim (2) is confused, for it gains what plausibility it has only through the fallacy of subreption. 'Somewhere' is a spatial predicate. And though it is true that anything which exists *empirically* exists in space, there are things (God might be an example) which exist non-spatially. These objects cannot, as the argument for the antithesis demonstrates, be known empirically. But they can be known rationally, by the use of Intellect alone.

So here, in the *Dissertation*, we have a curious mixture of Kant's new method and traditional metaphysical claims. Kant realises that our knowledge cannot be limited to mere empirical knowledge, for there are certain ordering principles presupposed by this very knowlege. These principles are known by Reason. We learn by experience, for example, that fire causes heat – Reason does not tell us this. But we do not learn by experience that every event has a cause. Rather we know it because the particular experiences we do have would be incoherent without it. So we may postulate rational knowledge in addition to empirical knowledge.

But an obvious question now arises: What are the ground rules for this sort of knowledge claim? How do we distinguish true intellectual claims from false ones, meaningful ones from nonsensical ones? Though we may agree that language limits the world (that is, conceptual intelligibility is a necessary condition for ontological possibility), we surely do not want to say that conceptual intelligibility is a sufficient condition for ontological actuality. In the *Dissertation*, Kant has little to say about this. He warns us not to limit metaphysical speculation by the demands of empirical knowledge, but he seems not to realise that he has opened a Pandora's box. Every claim of speculative metaphysics, whether about God or immortal souls or gremlins in my watch, now seems of equal worth. What Kant did not appreciate in the *Dissertation*, but what he comes to realise in the first *Critique*, is that the very principles rendering our experience comprehensible also put a limit upon the extent to which Reason alone (pure Reason) can competently pronounce. What begins in the *Dissertation* as an attempt to save rational metaphysics sows the seeds for its complete destruction. Hume's scepticism helped Kant to see this, but he had already started to see it in 1772. Part of Kant's 1772 letter to Marcus Herz is worth quoting here:

> In my dissertation I was content to explain the nature of intellectual representations in a merely negative way, namely, to state that they were not modifications of the soul brought about by the object. However, I silently passed over the further question of how a representation that refers to an object without being in any way affected by it can be possible. I had said: The sensuous representations present things as they appear, the intellectual representations present them as they are. But by what means are these things given to us, if not by the way in which they affect us? And if such intellectual representations depend on our inner activity, whence comes the agreement that they are supposed to have with objects – objects that are nevertheless not possibly produced thereby? And the axioms of pure reason concerning these objects – how do they agree with these objects, since the agreement has not been reached with the aid of experience?[4]

Kant has realised that we do have knowledge that is not merely written by experience on the *tabula rasa* of the mind. This knowledge is presupposed by experience, but not found in it. However, he now sees that he said nothing in the *Dissertation* which ruled out *any* rational speculative claim. For he had not lived up to his promise of providing principles of significance for the intellectual world. Though his question in the *Dissertation* was critical, his answer was not. The final answer, which will come in the first *Critique*, is that Reason's competence extends *only* to what is presupposed by experience – that when Reason pronounces

21

in total independence from experience it yields only nonsense. To explain why this is so, and to demonstrate the poverty arising in traditional metaphysics from not seeing that it is so, is the task of the first *Critique,* a critique of *pure* Reason – that is, Reason attempting to go it alone in complete independence of experience. The distinction Kant needs in the *Dissertation* but does not discover until later is that between *transcendental* claims (claims about what Reason discovers to be presupposed by experience) and *transcendent* claims (claims by Reason to knowledge beyond any consideration of experience). In the *Dissertation,* Kant seems to think that both are legitimate. In the first *Critique,* he realises that only the former are.

It was at this point, when Kant was already feeling doubts about Reason's unlimited competence, that he re-read Hume, a re-reading which he partially credited with awakening him from his dogmatic slumbers. Hume, for subtle and persuasive reasons, rejected – indeed ridiculed – just those sorts of metaphysical claims which Kant countenanced in the *Dissertation.* But he also rejected much more – even common-sense certainty and the knowledge of science. Thus Hume forced Kant to rethink his earlier and too easy answer to the question of metaphysical knowledge. Kant's rationalistic training made him realise that Locke and other empiricists were wrong in thinking our knowledge was limited to what could be experienced. Hume made him realise, however, that many of the traditional speculations of rational metaphysics were, to put it honestly, just plain silly. Kant sees that both rationalism and empiricism have an important story to tell, but that each exaggerates. The task of the critical philosophy, then, is to subject Reason to a critique of its own power to know so that a sober assessment of the contribution of both competing philosophical traditions can be made.

Now just what did Hume have to say that made such a great impression on the development of Kant's thought? Kant's philosophy is often popularly characterised as 'answering Hume', and so it will be useful to assess the precise nature of Hume's challenge, a challenge quite commonly misrepresented in courses on Kant.

Kant's first chance to become acquainted with Hume's early epistemological writings was in 1772, when Beattie's *Essay on the Nature and Immutability of Truth* was published in German translation. (Kant did not read English.) Hume's *An Enquiry Concerning Human Understanding* was translated in 1752, but Beattie's book provided extensive quotation from the *Treatise of Human Nature.* And it is the doctrine of the *Treatise,* and not that of the *Enquiry,* which causes Kant greatest concern. In both works Hume had raised fundamental questions about causality, often oversimplified by commentators in the claim that he denied that causal connection is necessary. Kant, then, it is often said, came along and showed (or at least asserted) that causal connection is necessary after all. This common claim is muddled, however, and failure to sort out the various issues involved in Kant's dispute with Hume is responsible for much misinterpretation of Kant. For it is important to distinguish two very different questions about causality: questions about particular causal connections (e.g. fire causes heat) and questions about the causal maxim or principle itself (every event has a cause). Hume denied the necessity of both, and Kant agrees fully with regard to the former. Heat, though caused by fire, could have been caused by something else. To find out what indeed causes heat, then, we have to conduct an empirical examination of the world. Reason will never tell us the answer to such a question, for (as Hume showed in the *Enquiry*) particular causal connections are not necessary. Given any causal connections like 'fire causes heat', it is always possible to deny the statement without absurdity. This would not be so if particular causal statements were necessary. So Kant has no answer to Hume on this point. He fully agrees with him.

On the necessity of the causal maxim, however, Kant believes that Hume's view in the *Treatise* is seriously mistaken. Hume argues that, just as it is possible without logical absurdity to deny the particular cause for any particular effect, so it is possible without logical absurdity to deny the claim that every event has a cause. It is not absurd (even if false) to suggest that heat might have had no cause at all. We have a disposition or habit to believe that every event must have a cause only because, according to Hume, we have never encountered an uncaused event. But there might be uncaused events anyway, and so the only necessity in the maxim is psychological – i.e. we cannot, given our mental associations, help believing the maxim.

This bothers Kant. For he is not at all sure that any sense can be given to the claim that there might be uncaused events. To deny that every event has a cause is not to contradict oneself, and so the maxim is not analytically necessary – that is, not true by definition.[5] But it seems necessary in another sense, in what I have previously called a transcendental sense. Unless one accepts the principle, our world will not be ordered at all, will not be susceptible of intelligible description. Suppose, for example, your friend's car broke down and, when you asked him what caused the breakdown, he replied that *nothing* caused it. It just broke down for no reason at all. You would surely think he was talking nonsense, not contradictory nonsense perhaps, but nonsense of some sort. For his claim would make the breakdown of the car absolutely inexplicable, would make it autonomous from the world in which you live. The breakdown of the car would become miraculous. We would be at a loss to know what to say about it. This would be very different from his claiming, for example, that its broken radio caused the car to stop running. This would merely be a false claim that we could correct by supplying a better explanatory candidate. But the suggestion that there was no cause or explanation at all is not just a false claim. It is nonsense. It transcends the range of remarks sensible to make about the world in which we live – a world of ordered connection between phenomena.[6]

Now why was Hume concerned to deny this principle, since it does seem necessary in some sense? The

24

claim that every event has a cause does not seem merely on a par with contingent empirical generalisations like 'All swans are white', for the claim 'There is an uncaused event' is shocking in a way that the claim 'There is a black swan' is not. But, with characteristic courage, Hume denies the principle anyway. And he does this because he accepts the following two principles, principles which Kant's critical philosophy is in part concerned to attack:

1. Whenever imagination perceives a difference among ideas it can easily produce a separation.
2. Whatever the mind conceives of clearly is possible.

Both of these claims occur in Section 3 (Book I, Part III) of the *Treatise*. Hume's argument against the necessity of the causal maxim then takes the following form: Since the event and its cause are different, we can (by 1) conceive of an event without conceiving of a cause. Thus (by 2) it is possible that something happens without a cause. But 'It is possible that not-p' is inconsistent with 'It is necessary that p'. Thus, since it is possible that something could happen without a cause, it cannot be necessary that every event has a cause.

This is the argument Hume leaves, and to challenge it is one of Kant's many purposes in writing the first *Critique*. Basically Kant will challenge Hume's claim (1), that the distinguishable is separable. The denial of this Humean position is the assertion of what Kant calls synthetic *a priori* connection – necessary connection (that is, connection true for all possible worlds) that is not analytic or definitional. The claim that we have synthetic *a priori* knowledge and the explanation of the possibility of such knowledge are the prominent themes of the *Critique of Pure Reason*. But the germ of an answer to Hume had already been latent in the *Dissertation's* distinction between sensible and intellectual knowledge. In the language of the *Dissertation*, Kant will charge Hume with the fallacy of subreption. For Hume's two principles are really principles only of sensible knowledge and are not to be regarded as conditions on the possibility of all knowledge. Thus all Hume has shown is that the causal maxim is not to be established empirically. To show how it is to be established, then, is one of Kant's major purposes in the first *Critique*.

In summary, we can now assess the state of Kant's thought prior to the publication of the *Critique of Pure Reason*. Kant realises that the teaching of the *Dissertation* is weak in its explication of the use of Intellect or Reason. He has opened the door to metaphysical nonsense. A possible move, of course, would have been to retreat to the claim that only empirical knowledge is possible, abandoning any claims to intellectual knowledge. But Hume had really blocked this move as well. For Kant is convinced that (i) empirical science, and not merely metaphysics, presupposes the causal principle or maxim and (ii) that no merely empirical analysis of this maxim (e.g. in terms of the association of ideas) is adequate. So Kant, who wants to claim that causal connection is both necessary and about the world, must begin a general examination of the role of Reason in knowledge. The examination yields his greatest work – the *Critique of Pure Reason*. Its general strategy, to use one of Lewis Beck's metaphors, will be to fight a two-front war against rationalism and empiricism. Empiricism, at least of the Humean variety, employs principles which would make any knowledge at all impossible. The logical outcome of empiricism is complete scepticism. But rationalism, though presenting a needed corrective to empiricist scepticism, is not itself sceptical enough. For, if left to its own devices, it defends the most preposterous claims. Thus there is great need to discover the legitimate use of Reason in the development of knowledge.

The Critical Philosophy

It would be ludicrous, in so short a compass in a book largely devoted to other topics, to attempt a summary of the infinitely complex thought of the

Critique of Pure Reason – a book made more complex by the fact that is is one of the most badly written books in the history of Western thought. All that I shall attempt to do here is to provide the reader with a sketch of some of the problems with which Kant was concerned to deal and to give the reader the flavour of that characteristic kind of argument which Kant calls transcendental.

Kant claims at the outset of the *Critique* that all previous philosophy suffered from being either sceptical or dogmatic. Sceptical philosophy, of the Humean variety, employed principles which have as their logical consequence the denial of what we all know in common sense, science and mathematics.[7] Hume indeed presents a *reductio* of his own view. If Hume is right, then common-sense knowledge, mathematical knowledge and scientific knowledge would not be possible. But they are actual, so they must be possible. Thus Hume must be wrong. Kant's problem, of course, is to diagnose the character of Hume's error without begging any of the important questions.

Dogmatic philosophy, by which Kant means speculative metaphysics of the rationalist variety, has quite a different weakness. The rationalists accept scientific and mathematical knowledge (though they too have their doubts about common sense) but provide no arguments to show how this knowledge is possible. Also, they tend to make extravagant and competing claims, making no use of any intelligible principles that might set standards for resolving their controversies. The rule in metaphysics seems to be that anything goes. As Hume had sagely observed, there is no thesis in philosophy so absurd that some metaphysician has not soberly propounded it.

Thus it seems obvious to Kant that philosophy stands in need of a new inquiry. It needs to become *critical* rather than sceptical or dogmatic. It is time to stop wasting time with such worries as whether or not my room continues to exist when I am not in it, on the one hand, and with gods and immortal souls on the other – at least until a preliminary inquiry has been got out of the way. This preliminary critical inquiry is just an examination of the faculty of Reason itself, a critique of Reason's own power to know. Each of Kant's major *Critiques* is devoted to an examination of Reason in one of its characteristic employments. The *Critique of Pure Reason* assesses Reason's contribution to theoretical knowledge – that found in science and mathematics, for example. The *Critique of Practical Reason* focuses upon Reason's employment in morality. The *Critique of Judgment* examines Reason's employment of the concept of purpose in art and nature. The main emphasis in the present work is on a part of Kant's practical philosophy. But a background in his theoretical philosophy, where he sets the ground rules for philosophical intelligibility, is a necessary prerequisite for a study of the rest of his system. Thus I shall briefly examine it here.

Now Kant claims that the mark of certain knowledge is the presence of strict universality or necessity – that is, truth in all possible worlds. Kant agrees with both the empiricists and the rationalists that this knowledge does not come solely from experience. We do not discover what is true for all possible worlds merely by observing what is true in one actual world. But from this premise the empiricist wrongly concludes that there is no such knowledge. And Kant claims that this is simply the denial of plain fact, for the knowledge that we have (for example) in empirical science presupposes certain *a priori* principles – like the principle that every event has a cause. But though these principles do not come from experience, they do not come solely from Reason either. For if they did, then any coherent flight of fancy would rate as metaphysical truth. Kant thus sees the importance of giving place to both of these competing claims. This is revealed in two of the most famous sentences in the first *Critique*:

Though all of our knowledge begins with experience, it does not follow that it all arises out of experience (B 1; Kemp Smith, 41).

Thoughts without content are empty; intuitions
28

without concepts are blind (A 51 = B 75; Kemp Smith, 93).

The view Kant is presenting here is simply this: Experience furnishes the materials of our knowledge, whereas the mind arranges these materials in a form made necessary by its own nature. This is not a claim of associationist psychology. Rather Kant is arguing that the coherent and intelligible description of the world which makes knowledge possible demands the employment of principles not susceptible of an analysis that is solely empirical in character. This is the view behind the claim that experience provides the matter or content of knowledge, whereas Reason provides its form. The mistake of the rationalists was to suppose that the mind originated the content of knowledge as well as the form (i.e. rationalism employs empty concepts). Kant says this is incorrect. The matter of knowledge is given – that is, we are passive in receiving it. But simply given data do not yet constitute knowledge (i.e. given data are blind intuition), for knowledge requires that the given in experience be coherently described through actively relating its parts according to intelligible principles. This gives it *wholeness,* in the language of the *Dissertation,* and transforms a confusion into an ordered world. To put it crudely, you can only know what you can say – what you can formulate into intelligible propositions.

The formal conditions which render this organisation of the given possible for knowledge are said to be contributed by Reason.[8] But you cannot have such formal organisation without content. Thus Reason is in no position to make claims about any entities lying beyond its content of given sensory experience. The mind merely provides organising principles, and organising principles must have something to organise in their legitimate employment. Thus Reason, though giving rise to non-empirical connections in the empirical given (what Kant calls the manifold of sensible intuition), is also limited to this given. The upshot is that the nature of our cognitive faculties explains how certain universal and necessary knowledge (e.g. every

29

event has a cause) is possible. But these same conditions demonstrate the impossibility of our ever having knowledge of what, if anything, is beyond experience. This is the basis of Kant's elimination of speculative metaphysics. In Kant's terminology, we can have transcendental knowledge of *phenomena* (*a priori* knowledge about conditions of possible experience), but no transcendent knowledge of *noumena* – that is, no knowledge of that beyond experience. Traditional speculative metaphysics is transcendent and noumenal, and thus hopeless. The only legitimate kind of metaphysics is, then, not a metaphysics beyond experience, but (in H. J. Paton's fine phrase) a metaphysics *of* experience. This, in summary, is Kant's contribution.

What is most intriguing, of course, are not these mere conclusions, but rather the subtle arguments that led Kant to adopt them. For it is in considering the characteristic Kantian arguments that one senses the power and depth of his philosophical procedure. And so it will be useful to explore one such argument by way of illustration: Kant's refutation of the Humean attack on the necessity of the causal maxim.

Kant's starting point against Hume is the realisation that we possess knowledge which, upon previous philosophical views, we could not possess. Traditionally, in for example Leibniz's distinction between truths of reason and truths of experience or Hume's distinction between relations of ideas and matters of fact, it was supposed that we had just two sorts of knowledge: necessary analytic knowledge and synthetic contingent knowledge. All necessary knowledge (claims true for all possible worlds) was thought to be analytic or true by definition, e.g. 'All bachelors are unmarried.' Synthetic knowledge (knowledge about the world rather than logic or language) was regarded as contingent, as discoverable only by experience, e.g. 'Water freezes at 32° F.' But what about a judgment like this:

Every event has a cause.

What is interesting about this judgment, according to Kant, is that it is both necessary and synthetic. That is, it is true in all possible worlds (and so necessary), but is about the world, about possible experiences, and is not merely a definition. Thus it is synthetic. You could, of course, decide to *make* the judgment analytic or true by definition, but Kant's point would then be to question how you know just what to build into the predicate of your new analytic claim. That you know just what to build in shows that you have necessary synthetic knowledge.[9] Kant called such judgments synthetic *a priori* judgments and argued that it was precisely these judgments that Hume and the empiricists could not account for. Indeed, Hume's principle that the distinguishable and the separable are identical is inconsistent with there being such judgments. For these judgments are just judgments in which the subject and predicate are distinguishable (because, being non-analytic, the predicate is not contained in the meaning of the subject) but not separable, since, for all possible worlds, they would go together. Kant, having noted the existence of these judgments, makes the central question of the first *Critique* the explanation of how they are possible and the explanation of their role in knowledge. Basically, he claims that their role in knowledge is to provide the limits of intelligible discourse about the world. They provide organising principles basic to our having any empirical knowledge. Since they organise experience, they do not come from experience. Rather they are found in Reason as a faculty which forms the matter of sensibility into an organised whole or world. Reason in this capacity Kant calls the faculty of Understanding. Though the idiom is that of faculty psychology, the philosophical point (as I have already argued) is not.

To appreciate Kant's philosophical point, it will be helpful to review what Hume had to say about the principle that every event has a cause. Hume's claim that this principle is not necessary is motivated, as we have seen, by a principle incompatible with the possibility of synthetic *a priori* judgments. According to Hume, we learn the causal principle as a habit by observing that certain events regularly go together in nature. This regular connection we call causal connection, and thus the only necessity in the causal maxim is an associationist or psychological necessity. That is, when confronted with some event E, we have a habit of expecting that we can find a cause for E. But it is possible that the event might have had no cause at all. Thus there is nothing epistemologically basic about the causal principle or maxim. We learn it by comparing and contrasting pairs of events, and we could dispense with it – though it is a useful habit not to.

Kant's strategy against this Humean account is to show that Hume's thesis gains its plausibility only by *presupposing the very principle whose necessity he is denying!* And this is a powerful answer indeed. Hume says we learn the causal principle by comparing events in nature. But, asks Kant, how do we distinguish an event? When is event language appropriate to apply to the world? It is only appropriate, claims Kant, when it is appropriate to apply the causal principle to the world, for this principle is criterial for events. The causal principle allows us to distinguish events in the first place, both from each other and from non-events, and thus Hume's claim that the causal principle is derived from the comparison of events (or better, can be analysed in terms of event association) cannot be correct.

Kant's argument comes out most clearly in the section of the first *Critique* called the 'Second Analogy' (A 189–211 = B 232–56; Kemp Smith, 218–33).[10] Here Kant raises the question of how we can distinguish an event (for example, a ship sailing down a river) from a non-event (for example, a house). What makes it appropriate to describe the first as an event but not the latter? Kant's answer is that the distinguishing mark of the first, and thus the distinguishing mark of an event, is the irreversibility of the time sequence involved in the perception of the object. Look, says Kant, at a ship sailing down a river and then, in imagination, reverse the order of your perceptions. You will find that what you are now imagining is a *different event*. But perceive a house from basement to roof. If you reverse the order of perception in imagination

32

(that is, imagine perceiving it from roof to basement) you will feel not the least temptation to claim that you are now perceiving another or different house. Now the manifestation of irreversible time order is just the manifestation of causality in nature. Thus the distinguishing mark of an event is the applicability of causality to it. And thus, in order to distinguish events, there is an epistemological necessity to apply the causal principle or maxim.

Kant's answer to Hume then is simply this: Hume is quite wrong in claiming that we develop the causal principle by habitually associating events. Rather the causal principle is employed in identifying events – those very things which Hume claims we associate. Thus, in Kant's idiom, empirical association has a transcendental ground. The very possibility of the kind of association Hume employs rests upon the acceptance of a synthetic *a priori* principle: Every event has a cause. Thus the principle is necessary, not contingent. It is presupposed by experience and is thus not itself empirically analysable. For the very discrimination to which Hume appeals in his argument to show that the causal principle is contingent can be made only if the causal principle is necessary. This is Kant's answer to Hume on causality. The answer is reached by a transcendental argument – an argument explaining the possibility of our being able to make a certain kind of judgment.

This then is the typical pattern of a transcendental argument: Consider some distinction we all make. We can make this distinction only on the presupposition of a certain synthetic *a priori* connection. This connection cannot come from experience, since experience presupposes it, and thus it must come from Reason in its capacity as Understanding – the faculty which provides the intelligible form for the sensible given in experience. Thus empirical knowledge is possible only because of the presence of a synthetic *a priori* connection provided by necessary organising principles. Kant calls these principles the *categories*. The categories, of which causality is one of twelve, are rules for the ordering of the manifold of intuition. Or, to put the point in non-Kantian language, they are rules which set the conditions for intelligible description of the world, the kind of descripton presupposed by science and common sense.

This, of course, is merely a very superficial overview of the nature of Kant's transcendental method. However, I hope that it at least serves the function of allowing the student to appreciate something of the kind of considerations which prompted Kant to reject empiricism of the Humean variety. Kant, as he is often interpreted, simply appears to beg the question against Hume – that is, he attempts to refute Hume by pressing claims which, if Hume were right, could not be correct. There is some of this in Kant, but there is also a much more subtle line of attack. For, at his best, Kant attempts to show that Hume tacitly employs just those *a priori* principles which he seeks to deny and that he *necessarily* employs them, as he could not draw his favourite distinctions without them.

Now, having rejected a thoroughgoing empiricism, Kant is by no means prepared to embrace, as he had done in the *Dissertation*, a system of speculative metaphysics. For he now comes to see that the principles of Reason which allow him to refute empiricism are such that, by their very nature, they cannot be employed outside of experience. For how are they discovered? Obviously, by a reflection upon experience and the presuppositions which make it possible. These principles, then, even though they are not themselves empirically analysable, arise in reflection on experience. They are, to use Kant's own term, *constitutive* of experience. That is, they make ordered experience possible through their active organisation of a manifold of intuition. This is the arena in which they get their sense. And there is no reason to suppose from this that Reason, since it is competent to pronounce on conditions of experience, is equally competent to pronounce on conditions totally beyond experience. Only Reason's transcendental competence has been established, not its transcendent competence.

Consider, with this in mind, the standard ontological entities of speculative metaphysics – entities like

34

God and immortal souls. The concepts of such entities cannot, according to Kant, serve a constitutive function. For their derivation is not in reflection upon the conditions for the possibility of experience, but rather simply from some metaphysical or theological grab-bag. They arise, as Kant says, from the *dialectical* employment of Reason. Reason, in its transcendental employment, discovers conditions for the possibility of experience. In its dialectical employment, however, Reason is pure. It attempts to go it alone, supplying the matter as well as the form of knowledge. And what does it yield thereby? Pure nonsense.

Kant thus makes quite a radical objection to speculative metaphysics. He does not believe that it is necessary to take up all speculative claims and attempt to refute them one by one (though he does consider many by way of illustration). Rather he thinks, in his role as philosophical therapist, that he has discovered the character of the metaphysical disease as it may manifest itself in any form and that he is therefore able (sometimes only by severely stretching his theory) to present a perfectly *general* refutation of all speculative or transcendent noumenal claims arising from the dialectical employment of Reason. Such claims are simply nonsensical. They do not even have the dignity of being false.[11]

Why is this so? Basically, Kant argues, it is because metaphysical philosophy, as traditionally practised, is guilty of *transcendental illusion*. This, very like the *Dissertation*'s fallacy of subreption, arises when locutions are used outside of that context of experience which gives them their sense. In a more contemporary idiom, we might say that the mistakes of speculative metaphysics are category or type mistakes. As Professor Ryle says in *The Concept of Mind,* one way of talking nonsense is uncritically to 'present the facts of one category in the idioms appropriate to another'. Ryle gives the example of a man who, having seen the buildings, grounds, students, administrators and faculty, is disappointed because he did not see that thing which is the university. This is nonsense, because the man asks of a general term questions only appropriate with regard to proper names.

Consider a sample metaphysical claim: God is the first cause of the universe. This claim is not contradictory and thus appears to have a sense. But this appearance is brought about only because there is a legitimate use of causal talk upon which the claim trades – phenomenal causation in experience. It is a context of experience which gives causal talk its life. When we analyse this claim about God, however, we see that it is employing causal talk *outside* that realm of experience which gives such talk intelligibility. And thus we have an assertion which literally has no sense, an assertion used with no attention to the kind of context which would render it sensible to make. For, upon close examination, what can we make of the notion of a first cause? If it is a cause, then it too must be a happening. But if it is a happening, it presupposes (by the causal maxim) a prior happening as its ground. But this would mean it could not be first. The only way to make it first would be to consider it not to be a happening, but then it could not be the sort of thing we understand as a cause. The claim is literally without sense; it is transcendentally silly. Such a cause would, if first, necessarily lie outside of experience. But if it were outside of experience, it could not be a cause. For causation, an *a priori* category of the Understanding, is just a rule of Understanding for the organisation of experience.

Kant thinks that here, then, is the general character of the metaphysical disease: the employment of concepts outside that context of experience which gives them their sense. Pure Reason seeks a final explanation of all the world – the unconditioned that lies behind all conditions. Such a condition, by its very specification, is outside the world and thus transcends the arena in which explanatory talk has its life. Such 'explanations' of pure Reason, since they are grammatically well formed, have the appearance of sense. But they are in fact completely vacuous.[12] The notions (God, immortal souls, first cause, etc.) arising from the metaphysical disease Kant calls Ideas. Categories are products of Reason rendering experience possible.

36

Ideas are products of Reason's dialectical employment in attempting to go beyond all experience. And to believe, as the speculative metaphysician believes, that Ideas have a constitutive employment, that they yield knowledge, is to be guilty of transcendental illusion. At most these Ideas have a regulative use as heuristic models around which to organise inquiry. Thus the upshot is that those very considerations which allowed Kant to discover Reason's legitimate employment in organising experience also yield the doomsday of speculative metaphysics. And this, simply, is Kant's great synthesis of rationalism and empiricism: the preservation of Reason's contribution in the absence of its preposterous claims to transcendent truth.

Kant's views are, of course, considerably more complex and closely argued than I have been able to suggest here. They are also, at least in parts, much more ambiguous and confusing. I have merely developed one major thrust of what is in reality a many-faceted epistemological and metaphysical theory. However, my purpose has been mainly to provide the epistemological-metaphysical background for Kant's moral philosophy. And two things of immediate consequence for his moral philosophy do come from this discussion. First, we should not be surprised to find Kant proceeding in an analogously transcendental way when examining morality. He will not attempt to discover a new morality. Neither will he spend much time in quelling the doubts of the moral sceptic. Rather he will start from the common-sense moral experience that we all have and will attempt to discover the presuppositions which make this experience coherent. And he will, not too surprisingly, lay most of the mistakes in moral philosophy at the door of empiricism. Second, in reacting against empiricism in ethics, he will not go to the other extreme and make speculative moral claims. That is, he will not (in the manner of Aquinas, for example) attempt to deduce moral conclusions from speculative metaphysical premises about God and his purposes for men. Such premises are nothing but metaphysical illusions. Reason's contribution in morality will be in discovering the conditions rendering our moral experience intelligible, allowing us to account for distinctions obscured by empiricism in ethics. Reason will not be employed, however, in the magical production of moral propositions from a morass of metaphysical and theological confusion.

The Character of Kant's Ethics

Kant's moral theory is best understood, at least initially, as a reaction against empiricism in ethics – particularly as a reaction against all forms of utilitarianism. Utilitarianism, though admitting of many diverse formulations, is basically to be characterised as an ethical theory which teaches that the fundamental right-making characteristic of morality (the answer to the question 'What makes a right act right?') is the promotion of, or at least the non-interference with, some *contingent* human value – that is, some value which human beings just happen, as a matter of fact, to desire. This value is discovered by an empirical examination of human nature and is typically taken to be happiness. The empirical character of this value is implicit in all utilitarian theories and is explicitly so characterised in many. Hume, for example, argues that reason can play no role in formulating the basic values of morality. Such values are set by 'the passions' and may be discovered only by an examination of what human beings do, as a matter of fact, prefer. Mill, in his famous 'proof' for the principle of utility, later argues in a similar way:

> The only proof capable of being given that an object is visible, is that people actually see it. The only proof that a sound is audible, is that people hear it: and so of the other sources of our experience. In like manner, I apprehend, the sole evidence it is possible to produce that anything is desirable, is that people do actually desire it. If the end which the utilitarian doctrine proposes to itself were not, in theory and in practice, acknowledged to be an end, nothing could

38

ever convince any person that it was so (*Utilitarianism*, chap. iv).

If we once grant that the basic value which places a limiting condition on the moral rightness of actions is discoverable by an empirical examination of human nature, it then follows that the actual business of ethics – the determining of moral duties – is also empirical in character. All we must do is discover what actions are causally instrumental to the attainment of this value. The task of philosophical ethics then becomes the quasi-scientific examination of effective *techniques* for maximising this value. And this explains the lengthy discussions of incentives and sanctions in most utilitarian theory. For even if we know that some type of action is most likely to maximise human happiness, we must still concern ourselves with the question of how we may guide (or, if necessary, goad) most people into performing actions of this type. Utilitarians, for example, are often prepared to argue – in an admittedly cynical fashion – that religious belief ought to be encouraged even if false because it can, if properly directed, provide strong incentives for the doing of right. For many people who will not ordinarily act morally can be goaded into doing so with the proper dose of hellfire and brimstone. In utilitarian theory, if not in practice, we find a large place occupied by the notion that the end justifies any means.

Kant has nothing but contempt for such proceedings in morality. And this is so for many reasons. First, and primarily, he wants to argue that such a conception of morality is incompatible with the basic *dignity* of human beings, beings set apart from all other natural creatures by their freedom – their capacity to act, at least some of the time, from reasons rather than from physical causes. To ground morality in some empirical value, in some merely contingent fact about human beings (e.g. their desire for happiness), is to obscure this essential character of humanity. For man is essentially a free and rational creature. Thus only some end set by reason can provide the basic value in a moral code that will respect man's dignity. Empirical values,

39

though discoverable for man, are also discoverable for any brute. Any animal could have, for its kind, a moral code of the kind utilitarianism envisions for man. This is the grain of truth in Nietzsche's later charge that utilitarianism is a pig philosophy. Thus Kant is concerned that morality be not grounded in some contingent value, like happiness, that men happen to desire. Rather he seeks to ground morality in a value which gives man his own worth. Men, though desiring happiness, do not derive their dignity or worth from desiring it. For the most debased of creatures could be imagined who would desire their own happiness. Rather, according to Kant, men derive their worth from *freedom*, the characteristic which essentially distinguishes man from any other creature in nature.

Kant's second crucial objection against utilitarianism is not merely that it picks the wrong value, but that in picking such a value the utilitarian theory allows itself to entail the most obviously immoral consequences. Kant indeed was one of the first to raise what is now the classic objection to utilitarianism: that it is incompatible with *justice*. For one can imagine the utilitarian principle being used to justify the most obviously unjust, and therefore immoral, conduct. Slavery, for example, could be justified on the grounds that the misery of a few slaves is more than compensated for by the happiness of the slaveholders. Or, even if some utilitarian should argue that this is never factually the case, such a move still seems without moral relevance, since it seems morally perverse even to *consider* the advantages of the slaveholder in the first place – since, whatever he gets, he gets unjustly.[13] Kant makes similar objections to the utilitarian view that it is morally permissible to punish an innocent man for the good of all or that it is permissible to interfere with the freedom of primitive peoples for 'their own good':

It might seem that there is ample justification for the use of violent means [against primitive peoples] because of the good for mankind that results from it.

On the one hand it is a means of bringing culture to primitive peoples (this is like the excuse that Büsching offers for the bloody introduction of Christianity into Germany), or, on the other hand, it is a means by which it is possible to clean out vagrants and criminals from one's own country, who, it is hoped, will improve themselves or their children in some other part of the world.... Nevertheless, all these good intentions still cannot wash away the stains of injustice from the use of such means (*Metaphysical Elements of Justice*, 353; Ladd, 126. Hereinafter, this work will be cited simply as *Justice*).[14]

Thus Kant is concerned to argue that utilitarianism presents an oversimplified – indeed perverse – picture of the subtleties of our common moral experience. Kant himself ultimately finds an important place for happiness in his own theory, but the notion that happiness is the supreme or overriding value in morality strikes him as absurd.

Now at this point, one may be inclined to ask the following question: Is it not simply begging the question on Kant's part to attempt to ground morality in reason instead of emotion? How can he demonstrate that reason ought to be taken so seriously as to deserve a chief place in moral philosophy?

Kant has an answer to this worry. With regard to the question, how does one defend the primacy of reason, it is important to note that the question may itself enshrine a certain muddle. For if Kant is being asked to defend reason, one would suppose that he is being asked to give *reasons* for valuing rationality. But this is paradoxical. If the person asking the question is prepared to listen to reasons seriously, this shows his question (since he already does value rationality) lacks a point. If he is not prepared to listen to reasons, one wonders what he could mean by asking for a defence or justification.

However, the question may be reformulated so as not to involve this absurdity. Perhaps the worry is not over whether or not reason is a value, but over whether or not reason should be taken as having a decisive role in *morality*. This question is not only sensible, but it is very difficult to answer. For though one may value rationality (listen to reasons and take them seriously), one may still wish to argue that the possession by a man of rationality has little to do with his moral worth, or with the applicability of moral evaluation to his action.

Kant's answer to this worry involves some of the basic assumptions of his entire ethical theory. Quite generally, Kant's argument that morality is to be founded on rationality takes the following form: Morality makes sense only if men are free; freedom is just the ability to act from reasons; thus morality will make sense only if it is grounded on rationality.

What is Kant's basis for asserting the two premises? The first premise, the famous claim that 'ought' implies 'can', is presented by Kant in the *Critique of Pure Reason*:

> That our reason has causality, or that we at least represent it to ourselves as having causality, is evident from the *imperatives* which in all matters of conduct we impose as rules upon our active powers. 'Ought' expresses a kind of necessity and of connection with grounds which is found nowhere else in the whole of nature. The understanding can know in nature only what is, and has been, or will be. We cannot say that anything in nature *ought to be* other than what in all these time relations it actually is. When we have the course of nature alone in view, 'ought' has no meaning whatever. It is just as absurd to ask what ought to happen in the natural world as to ask what properties a circle ought to have (A 547 = B 575; Kemp Smith, 472–3).

It is not clear that Kant is here claiming anything so strong as that statements of the form 'You ought to do so and so' logically entail statements of the form 'You can do so and so.' But he is at the very least claiming that statements of the former sort are practically *pointless*, without intelligible function, if the latter statements are always false. For moral demands are imperatives. And this is why morality – so full of

42

advice, injunction, admonition, praise and blame – would be absurd if people were not free. It may not be contradictory to blame a stone for falling on your head, but it is certainly inappropriate and pointless. So Kant's view is that moral evaluation makes sense only if directed to free agents.[15]

The second premise is Kant's attempt to distinguish human freedom from mere chance. We are tempted to say that what distinguishes human behaviour from the behaviour of inanimate objects like stones is that the behaviour of the latter, but not all the behaviour of the former, is causally predictable in principle. But this will not do. For then molecules, colliding in a statistically random way, would be free in the morally requisite sense. And this is absurd. So, in order to distinguish human freedom from the freedom of chance, Kant introduces the notion of rationality. Human behaviour is essentially different from the behaviour of all other objects in the world because it is explainable (unlike the random position of a molecule) but is not always causally explainable (unlike the behaviour of stones). Rather it is often explainable in terms of *reasons*. Human beings, though sometimes caused to do what they do (John sat on the pin and jumped up), often perform actions from reasons or purposes. Why did John go to the bank? *In order to* cash a cheque. This at least appears to be a very different kind of explanation from a causal explanation like 'because he was carried in'. So human action may be called free to the extent that it is explainable in terms of reasons.[16]

So Kant's whole ethical theory is, to use his own phrase, an attempt to discover *laws of freedom* – that is, rational principles for the intelligent direction of the activities of free beings. Anything less would not count as morality at all, but would at most be a sociological description of how people *do* behave, not a normative prescription about how they, as free agents, *ought* to behave:

If moral philosophy were nothing but eudaemonism [the happiness theory], it would be absurd to look for a priori principles for help. However plausible it

43

might seem that reason, even before experience, could discern by what means one can attain lasting enjoyment of the true joys of life, nevertheless everything that is taught a priori on this subject is either tautological or assumed without any ground. Only experience can teach us what brings us joy.... But it is otherwise with the instructions of morality. They command everyone without regard to his inclinations, solely because and insofar as he is free and has practical reason. Instruction in the laws of morality is not drawn from observation of oneself and the animality within him nor from the perception of the course of the world as to how things happen and how men in fact do act.... But reason commands how one ought to act, even though no such instance of such action might be found.... Indeed, concepts and judgments concerning ourselves and our actions and omissions have no moral significance at all if they contain only what can be learned from experience. Anyone so misled as to make into a basic moral principle something derived from this source would be in danger of the grossest and most pernicious errors (*Justice*, 215–16; Ladd, 15–16).

Thus far, then, I have claimed the following: Kant's own characterisation of morality demands that the values regarded as ultimate be set by reason, not by sensuous inclination. If (as in utilitarianism) they are set by inclination, then they are not products of freedom. They are, in Kant's terminology, heteronomous rather than autonomous. Morality is necessarily a system of laws of freedom, telling what ends free agents ought to adopt and how free agents ought to behave with respect to these ends; it is not a description of how people actually do behave (e.g. prefer happiness). This is what essentially distinguishes moral talk from sociological generalisation. And this is Kant's basic point against any form of utilitarianism: its ultimate value is not rationally justifiable at all. It merely describes the behaviour of people. Ultimately, utilitarianism is not a moral theory at all. It is merely sociology.[17]

44

An appreciation of Kant's anti-empirical, anti-utilitarian orientation allows his reader to understand the large role played in his ethical theory by the notion of 'what the fully rational being would do'. Kant's supreme principle of morality, his famous Categorical Imperative, is just a description of fully rational action. However, it is important to realise that Kant (unlike, say, Aquinas) does not hold that there really are fully rational beings and that their plans for men provide a definition of what is and what is not morally good. Rather he merely employs the concept of the fully rational being to explain, in a rather powerful manner, exactly what is the nature of his divergence from empiricism in ethics.

Thus the concept of a fully rational being is, for Kant, a model of explanatory value in characterising ideals of rational decision for human beings.[18] Its closest analogue is to be found not in any theological notions but in the notions of the 'economic man' employed, for example, in consent and decision theory. It is an ideal explication of the intuitively comprehensible, but generally unanalysed, notion of rational decision. Kant, accepting a Humean dichotomy between reason and the passions, characterises a fully rational being as one whose reasons for acting are *never* to be found in an appeal to desires or sensuous inclinations. Human beings, of course, are not like this. But Kant's point is that human actions are moral (because rational) only in so far as they do not find their justification in appeal to sensuous inclination or desire. And this is because it is only by acting in this way (analogous, in so far as possible, to the way a fully rational being would act) that man reveals his dignity – asserts that autonomy which distinguishes him from the brutes. So when Kant, in his *Foundations of the Metaphysics of Morals*, asserts the primacy of the good will in morality, he is in effect telling us that the principles of morality bind, not because we desire the ends attained by them, but because they are the sort of principles that a being of good will (that is, a fully rational will) would adopt.

This is what Kant means in claiming that the de-

45

mands of morality are *categorical*.[19] He is not, as some people have foolishly supposed, making the point that moral principles must take a categorical rather than an hypothetical grammatical form. This is not even true, and would be trivial if it were true. 'If you make a promise, then keep it' is a categorical moral demand according to Kant, even though it is expressed in an hypothetical grammatical form. And by this he means that our obligation to abide by the principle depends in no way upon our desire or lack of desire for the end that the principle, if adopted, would obtain. This differs from, for example, 'If you want to get to the airport in the fastest time, then take a taxi.' For this imperative consequence binds us (is the rational thing to do) only on the assumption that the end in question is indeed one which is desired. If I am in no hurry to get to the airport, then it is silly to tell me that I ought to take a taxi. So the demands of morality are categorical rather than hypothetical, not because of their grammatical form, but because they constitute rational principles of action even in the absence of any desire for the consequence to be brought about. My obligation to keep my promises, for example, in no way depends upon whether or not I *desire* to perform those actions which constitute keeping them. But my prudential obligations (e.g. 'I ought to take a taxi') bind only if I desire the end to which they are means. This is what Kant means in calling them hypothetical. Indeed, the terms 'categorical' and 'hypothetical' do not really modify the demands or imperatives in question at all. Rather they modify the *relation* that the demands bear to the *will* of the agent. If they bind even if not desired (or undesired), they are categorical.[20]

> All imperatives *command* either hypothetically or categorically. The former present the practical necessity of a possible action as a means to achieving something else which one desires (or which one may possibly desire). The categorical imperative would be one which presented an action as of itself objectively necessary, without regard to any other end (*Foundations*, 414; Beck, 31, italics added).

46

Now the attempt to determine principles definitive of what the fully rational being would do constitutes what Kant calls his *pure* or *formal* moral philosophy. These principles are pure in two senses. First, they are strictly universal — that is, they hold for all possible worlds intelligible to reason. Utilitarian considerations, on the other hand, would apply only to some worlds, i.e. worlds inhabited by creatures who desired happiness. However, it is possible to imagine worlds inhabited by creatures of whom it would be true to say both that (i) we owed them moral duties and (ii) they did not desire happiness. Our duties to God would be of this sort. And thus there is a kind of obligation claim that makes perfectly good sense but would not make sense on a utilitarian model.

The principles are also pure in another sense: they cannot be discovered by an empirical examination of nature. This is so for the obvious reason that one cannot discover principles holding for all possible worlds by examining what, in fact, obtains in one actual world. One will not expect then that Kant will follow the enterprise countenanced (at least tacitly) by the utilitarians of doing surveys and taking polls to find what things are or are not of moral value. This could at most discover what human beings do in fact desire, not what they — as rational beings — ought to desire.

At this point one is bound to get suspicious of Kant's entire enterprise. For what one now expects, if one is familiar with the traditional muddles of non-empirical ethical theory (e.g. natural law theory), is some hopeless appeal to intuition or rational inspection or even faith. One will expect Kant to play the traditional role of moral magician by plucking ethical ends out of a theological or metaphysical hat.

Happily, however, this is not what one finds in Kant at all. He does not, in a utilitarian fashion, attempt to discover basic moral values by recording the frequency of certain kinds of preferences. Nor, like the classical moral metaphysician, does he attempt to arrive at these values by showing that they follow from theological or metaphysical premises of dubious credentials. His method is neither inductive nor deductive.

47

Rather, as one acquainted with the *Critique of Pure Reason* might expect, he argues for these values by a *transcendental* argument. A transcendental argument or deduction, it will be recalled, proceeds from experience to a discovery of those conditions making this experience possible. It discovers presuppositions or necessary conditions for intelligibility. We do not discover in experience that every event has a cause. But unless we make this supposition, the experience we do have would not be possible – that is, would not be susceptible of intelligible description.

Similarly in morality. We do not discover that freedom is a value by inductive argument. We do not note that people say things like 'Freedom is a good thing' with great frequency. Rather, we see that unless freedom is *presupposed* as a basic value, much of our ordinary moral talk – that which it is the business of the moral philosopher to analyse – would not make sense, would not be intelligible. When we look at paradigm instances of common-sense moral justification, we realise that this justification – indeed the whole notion of justification itself – would make no sense unless we recognise that interference with freedom always stands in need of justification. This is particularly true with regard to that sphere of moral talk concerned with *rights*. The central question 'By what right?' gets its life only in the realisation that interference with freedom, bad in itself, is always open to challenge:

> When a controversy arises over an acquired right and the question is raised as to who has the burden of proof – either with respect to a disputed fact or, if this is settled, with respect to a disputed right – someone who denies this obligation [to prove his case] can methodically appeal to his innate right of freedom as though he were invoking various titles of right (*Justice*, 238; Ladd, 44).[21]

Thus Kant's whole conception of morality and moral philosophy is closely tied to our common-sense moral beliefs and the patterns of justificatory arguments which give them expression. He is not attempting to give us a new morality. But neither is he concerned, as is the empiricist, merely to record expressions of moral belief. Such a task is scientific and not philosophical at all. Kant's concern is rather to take these expressions as data, much as scientific judgments are taken as data in epistemology, and he sees the business of philosophy to be the discovery of those conditions which render these data intelligible. A basic moral principle, then, will be one presupposed by common moral talk. And one does not discover presuppositions for intelligibility by empirical surveys.

So Kant, as I have previously observed, is not himself a sceptic and is not to be regarded as answering the sceptic. He never doubts that we have moral knowledge (he calls this a 'fact of reason') or that we have empirical knowledge. His task is to explain the possibility of this knowledge. And this possibility is explained by discovering *a priori* principles underlying whole bodies of discourse and rendering this discourse intelligible. Kant's pure or formal moral philosophy, then, may be regarded as an attempt to discover the principles presupposed by our common moral experience which render that experience coherent and intelligible. And these principles are, according to Kant, best explicated in terms of the model of what the fully rational being would do:

> I have adopted in this writing the method which is, I think, most suitable if one wishes to proceed analytically from common knowledge to the determination of its supreme principle and then synthetically from the examination of this principle and its sources back to common knowledge where it finds its application.... [But from the fact that] we have derived our concept of duty from the common use of our practical reason, it is by no means to be inferred that we have treated it as an empirical concept. On the contrary, if we attend to our experience of the way men act, we meet frequent and ... justified complaints that we cannot cite a single sure example of the disposition to act from pure duty.... [Still]

without in the least teaching common reason anything new, we need only to draw its attention to its own principles, in the manner of Socrates, thus showing that neither science nor philosophy is needed in order to know what one has to do in order to be honest and good.... The most remarkable thing about ordinary reason in its practical concern is that it may have as much hope as any philosopher of hitting the mark (*Foundations*, 392, 404–6; Beck, 8, 20–2).

Now in addition to a pure moral philosophy, Kant also has an applied or *material* moral philosophy. Here, particularly in his book *The Metaphysics of Morals*, the formal principles of the pure moral philosophy are applied to the special requirements of a partially rational being like man in order to characterise particular classes of duties. We might know what a fully rational maxim for a holy will would be like without knowing what, in special human circumstances, would *count* as the closest approximation to such a maxim. Principles for the conduct of fully rational beings are obviously going to apply only by way of analogy to partially rational beings. Thus the task of the material moral philosophy will be the attempt to supplement the formal moral philosophy with what Kant calls anthropological knowledge of man's nature in order to formulate a moral criterion applicable to creatures of his sort. When confronted with a complex human situation, it would be of precious little help merely to tell me to act like a fully rational being. Presumably a fully rational being would not get himself into characteristically human muddles in the first place. Thus I shall want to know what, given the finite character of my own situation, I can do which will realise, in so far as is humanly possible, rationality in my situation. And the metaphysics of morals, as distinct from the foundations for such a metaphysics, will supposedly be of aid here.

Before beginning a detailed examination of Kant's formal and material moral philosophy as it bears on right actions, it will be helpful to close this chapter with a brief explanation of some of Kant's technical distinctions between kinds of duties. This will enable the reader to understand the focus of my discussion in the body of the book.

Kant's initial classification of duties, in the *Foundations of the Metaphysics of Morals*, is into duties to self and duties to others. These duties can be either perfect or imperfect. A duty is imperfect if no one is in a position to demand by *right* that it be complied with. I have, according to Kant, a duty to promote human happiness. This duty is imperfect, however, because no one can demand by right that I make him happy, can regard himself as wronged if I fail to make him happy. The contrast here is with a perfect duty like the duty to honour a contract. Here the person to whom I am bound in contract can demand by right that I honour it, can legitimately regard himself as wronged if I fail to honour it. 'By what right did you break your contract?' is a perfectly legitimate complaint, whereas 'By what right did you refuse to make me happy?' normally is not, since presumably I do not need to justify ignoring Jones's unhappiness as I would need to justify not honouring a contract with him.[22] Thus the duty to honour a contract is perfect. A duty is a duty to self if the agent is himself its object, e.g. the duty not to commit suicide and the duty to perfect my moral and natural personality. To the extent that others are affected, then these duties may also be duties to others. Kant's point, however, is that they remain duties that I owe myself even if, as a matter of fact, no others are affected at all.

These distinctions allow us to explain those duties which are, according to Kant, a proper part of political ethics. Political ethics concerns *perfect duties to others*. Kant's term for these duties is *juridical* duties or duties of justice. Political duties are those duties which are, at least *prima facie*, a proper object of coercion by the

State. And it would be impossible for the State to enforce my duties to self. What, for example could the State do to make me develop a morally praiseworthy character, e.g. love for my fellow men? The coercive machinery of State law is efficacious only with regard to external actions, not with regard to personal dispositions.[23] This point is important to a proper assessment of the force of moral legislation. Civil rights legislation, for example, cannot make bigots love black people, but only *treat* them in ways that are just. And politically this is quite enough. Further moral demands, demands for certain feelings or dispositions, Kant calls ethical duties or duties of virtue. And these duties have no relevance to political ethics, this being concerned solely with juridical duties.

But what about imperfect duties to others? Kant admits that the State would be able to enforce these, but argues that it would be morally wrong for the State to do so. The function of the State, as Kant conceives it, is to adjudicate competing claims of right between citizens – to replace violence with a just social decision procedure: the Rule of Law. But no man may justifiably claim the performance of an imperfect duty as he can the performance of a perfect duty. A man is wronged if I break a contract with him, but not wronged if I merely fail positively to promote his happiness. I may violate his rights by interfering with his happiness,[24] but not by simply ignoring it. It is for this reason, then, that Kant confines the sphere of political ethics to perfect duties to others.

Let me put Kant's point another way: Law is justified only to the extent that it preserves the freedom of all beings affected by it. Legal coercion is justified only to secure freedom. Only if I unjustly limit another man's freedom is the State justified in restraining me through the coercive machinery of its force. Now if I enter into a contract with a man, we both agree to limit our freedom for mutual benefit. If I break the contract, however, I have interfered with the freedom of my co-contractor because he experiences the limitation on his freedom contained in the contract without enjoying that benefit which, to his mind at least, justified this limitation. Contracts restrict the freedom, reduce the options, of their participants. Thus he has a right (traceable to his right to freedom) to seek redress – to demand that the State coerce me into honouring the contract or, if this is too late, to compensate him for losses sustained. The man who is simply unhappy has no comparable claim against me. I have not violated his freedom. I have merely exercised my right to leave him alone.

Having outlined the preliminaries necessary for an understanding of Kant's moral and political thought, I shall now pass to a detailed examination of the major topic of the present study: Kant's philosophy of right.

Introduction

One of the most characteristic things about human beings is that they are purposive creatures. They have plans and projects (Kant would call these *maxims*) and, if they are at all rational, they will consider which of these they ought or ought not to translate into action. And thus it is characteristic and important that people consider the kinds of *justification* to which their plans are susceptible. In so far as a man is rational, he will not act in the absence of a sufficient justification. There are all sorts of good reasons or justifications for acting, and the kind of man I am is often revealed in the kind of reasons I take most seriously. If the justification which most moves me to perform an action is that it is in my own interest, I am a man of prudence. If the reasons are in terms of the cultivation of certain subjective states, I may be an aesthete or a voluptuary. Relevant reasons define alternative points of view from which the world may be perceived and acted upon.

Now one sort of reason for acting, often placed in contrast to self-interest or desire, is the notion of duty or obligation. To take such a notion most seriously as a reason is to adopt towards the world and my actions in it a *moral* point of view. As a social institution, morality functions primarily to thwart inclination. And even when duty and inclination coincide, we can all see that 'It is in my interest to do *A*' or 'I desire to do *A*' are very different claims from 'It is my moral duty to do *A*'. So, when I am concerned over whether a planned action is morally permissible (right) or required (obligatory), I am concerned with whether or not the action can be defended with the right sort of reasons – those reasons definitive of the moral point of view.[1] And thus it is no surprise that the leading task of philosophical ethics, from ancient times to the present, has been the attempt to characterise just those reasons which are of the essence of morality.

Kant is no exception. His Categorical Imperative, his 'supreme principle of morality', is essentially an attempt to characterise the kind of justification to which a plan or maxim must be susceptible if I am to be morally justified in putting it into practice. And when the principle is understood in this way, it is no surprise and certainly no objection that it is in some sense a *formal* principle – that is, specified without regard to the particular purposes that people have. Purposes come from people's plans or maxims (what they intend to do), and the Categorical Imperative serves to *test* these purposes in order to determine if acting on them would be morally permissible. One takes maxims of action to the Categorical Imperative to determine if they are morally valid, much as one takes litigation to a judge to determine if it is legally valid. But the Categorical Imperative is itself no more a source of maxims or purposes than a judge is a source of litigation. And since we do not normally object for this reason that judges are useless because their function is formal, we should not object to the Categorical Imperative for such reasons either.

Now very roughly, my plans or maxims can be of various types. Either other people or my own person can be the object of my plans, and this gives Kant his distinction between duties to others and duties to self. Also, my plans can be to act in certain ways or to adopt certain feelings, motives or general ends; and this gives Kant his distinction between a theory of right or justice and a theory of virtue. Since my concern is with that part of morality often called social or political ethics, I shall consider the Categorical Imperative only in so far as it bears on the theory of right with regard to duties to others. Even with this limitation, however, the interpretation of the Categorical Imperative remains a rather complex enterprise. It is often said that Kant, above all other philosophers, perpetually succeeds in being technical without being precise. And this sour judgment, I am afraid, holds for his famous supreme principle of morality.

The Categorical Imperative

Perhaps no other aspect of Kant's moral philosophy generates quite so much confusion as his attempt to arrive at what he calls 'the supreme principle of morality'. It is hard to reach agreement, not only concerning whether or not it works, but even over what it is and what it is supposed to do. For, as A. R. C. Duncan has pointed out,[2] the phrase 'supreme principle *of* morality' is ambiguous in an important sense – especially in a Kantian context. It could mean a principle *within* morality (a moral principle proper) of a fundamental nature. On this interpretation, it would serve somewhat the same function as Mill's principle of utility – a single principle by which all other moral principles could be determined. However, the phrase could also mean a non-moral principle which is supreme in the sense of being an important *presupposition* or necessary condition for morality. We might, for example, claim that the truth of the statement 'Man has free will' is a necessary condition for or a supreme principle of morality. This latter kind of claim would be perfectly at home in Kant's philosophy, for he is often interested in discovering the presuppositions of certain facts. In the *Foundations*, for example, Kant claims that the Principle of Antonomy is the supreme principle of morality.

Thus, in dealing with the Categorical Imperative, we must address ourselves to the following question: Is the Categorical Imperative a metaethical principle or is it a principle of normative ethics? That is, is it an attempt to analyse the nature and presuppositions of morality or is it a piece of high-level moral advice? The answer is that it is *both*. For, considering for just a moment the first formulation, Kant uses the expression 'the Categorical Imperative' ambiguously to mean either of the following:

CI$_1$: Act only according to that maxim by which

57

you can at the same time will that it should become a universal law (*Foundations*, 421; Beck, 39).

CI_2: Act as though the maxim of your action were by your will to become a universal law *of nature* (ibid., italics my own).

In the *Foundations*, Kant treats these two as though they are really equivalent, and many of his commentators make the same mistake. Indeed, H. J. Paton was really the first to see how important it is to keep the distinction between CI_1 and CI_2 straight. For, as Kant himself points out in the *Critique of Practical Reason*, the principle CI_2 (with its stress on *nature*) is really CI_1 provided with a model or *typic* for application to the moral requirements of humanity. Though my purpose in this chapter is to examine CI_1 as an attempt on Kant's part to analyse the moral point of view, it will be useful to present a brief outline of the relationship between CI_1 and CI_2 as I conceive it. This will serve to locate my discussion of CI_1 in the context of Kant's theory of right as a whole.

My general interpretation is that the Categorical Imperative in the first sense (CI_1) states a description of the conditions that are necessary and sufficient for *any code of conduct that would count as a rational morality*. In its two other formulations, CI_1 outlines the general role of *ends* in morality without regard for the specific material content of any particular end, i.e. without regard for contingent objects of desire. In all its formulations, CI_1 is a pure principle, devoid of any empirical content whatsoever. It is merely descriptive of perfect rationality and can alone provide no fully adequate criterion of rightness for humanity. However, when provided with a typic, CI_1 becomes CI_2 and thereby does provide a moral criterion for rightness of actions. A typic makes use of certain empirical facts about man's nature and purposes such that the question 'What is rational action *for men*?' can be answered. CI_1 simply tells us that any rational being must will only actions that are consistent with the demands of rationality in general. But it does not tell us what, in particular cases, *counts* as being rational. And, in fact, it could not do this. For we as men can be rational only with respect to our ends and purposes. And unless such ends are given, the notion of 'being rational' remains vacuous for all practical purposes. All rational beings are purposive creatures and thus have ends, but for rational beings *in general* the notion of end or purpose must be a variable. It is for this reason that, in stating the supreme moral principle for *all* rational beings, Kant cannot state it in terms of arbitrary or contingent ends. Human nature, however, fixes certain ends. And thus human rationality is in part to be characterised in relation to the proper pursuit of those ends. CI_1 tells us that, in order to be a part of a rational morality, a maxim must be universalisable. But this is not yet a moral criterion for us, because it does not provide complete guidance in determining whether or not a particular maxim is universalisable. To know this latter, I must know some facts about human nature. (For example, whether or not I act immorally in hoarding a certain commodity – candy or oxygen, say – will depend in part on such empirical facts as its scarcity and the extent to which it is needed or desired by other people.)

Now this general interpretation will need expansion and defence. And I intend to devote this and the following chapter to providing just that. In this chapter, I shall consider the Categorical Imperative as a pure principle (CI_1). I shall argue that this principle serves for Kant the metaethical function of characterising the sphere of morality. In the following chapter, I shall discuss the Categorical Imperative provided with a typic (CI_2). I shall argue that this principle is a normative moral criterion, that it provides moral guidance for a particular rational being – man.

Now the distinction between ethics and metaethics is, as distinctions go in philosophy, fairly new. Metaethics is really a self-conscious twentieth-century enterprise which, though it was pursued implicitly by earlier philosophers (e.g. Hume), was seldom explicitly and never under the name 'metaethics' pursued prior to our own day. The term 'metaethics' has, until some-what recently, been taken to mean any analysis of the meaning or function of moral language. Thus such views as 'emotivism' (C. L. Stevenson) and 'cognitiv-ism' (G. E. Moore) are properly called metaethical. They tell us, not what we ought to do, but what moral language means or how moral language functions. Though I think that Kant has some definite opinions on these issues, an examination of these opinions is not germane to my present purpose.

More recently, however, metaethics has concerned itself with a very different sort of problem: the attempt to define or characterise the sphere of morality itself, to analyse the 'moral point of view' and to show how it differs from other points of view like the aesthetic, the prudential and the economic. The works of such writers as Toulmin, Hare, Baier and Singer can all be viewed as, at least in part, such attempts.[3] The issue that essentially divides these men is the question whether the moral point of view can be given a strictly formal characterisation (e.g. in terms of consistency) or whether it must be defined in terms of particular ends or purposes or even values, e.g. social harmony. I shall call metaethical theories of the former sort 'formalist' and those of the latter sort 'teleological'.[4] And my general argument will be that Kant, though often classed with the former, has important affinities with the latter.

Now it is my view that Kant's conception of a 'pure' moral philosophy is essentially just this: an attempt to describe necessary and sufficient conditions that any code of conduct – whether divine, angelic or human – must meet if that code is to count as a rational moral-ity. His concern in pure moral philosophy is to answer the question 'What in general is characteristic of rational conduct?' Morality is a practical activity, em-ploying rational principles that lead to action. Thus pure moral philosophy concerns itself with spelling out necessary and sufficient conditions that must be met by any action if it is to be correctly judged as *fully* rational. Kant is well aware that being fully rational is an unattainable Ideal for man, but this does not concern the problems of pure moral philosophy. For pure moral philosophy (unlike the metaphysics of morals) is not interested in applying principles to man or any other *particular* rational being. Rather it seeks to answer the prior question of what counts as *ideally* rational decision and conduct:

> But since moral laws should hold for every rational being as such, the principles must be derived from the universal concept of a rational being generally. In this manner all morals, which need anthropology for their application to men, must be completely developed first as pure philosophy.

> [We must first] investigate the idea and principles of a possible pure will and not the actions of the human volition as such, which are for the most part drawn from psychology (*Foundations*, 412, 390; Beck, 28, 7).[5]

Kant's actual analysis of what counts as fully rational action in general is surprisingly simple and straightforward. But, as we might expect, discussion of Kant's actual views must be preceded by clearing the ground of terminological confusion. For though Kant carefully distinguishes between the *pure* part and the merely *a priori* part of morality, he often mixes up the two when he is not being careful. In the *Critique of Pure Reason*, Kant gives us the following characterisation:

> We shall understand by *a priori* knowledge, not knowledge independent of this or that experience, but knowledge absolutely independent of all experience. Opposed to this is empirical knowledge, which is knowledge through experience, that is *a posteriori*. *A priori* modes of knowledge are entitled *pure* when there is no admixture of anything empirical. Thus, for instance, the proposition 'every alteration has its cause', while an *a priori* proposition, is not a pure proposition, because alteration is a concept which can be derived only from experience (B 3; Kemp Smith, 43).

A pure principle, then, is a principle which satisfies two conditions:

1. All concepts employed in it are *a priori* in origin.
2. All the connections between these concepts are *a priori*.

An example of such a pure principle would be the claim 'God is perfectly good'. Neither the subject nor predicate terms in this claim have their origin in experience (God and perfect goodness are not empirical concepts), and the connection between 'God' and 'perfect goodness' is analytic and thus *a priori*. A mere *a priori* principle, on the other hand, is one whose concepts may be empirical so long as the connections between these concepts are *a priori*, i.e. necessary and not contingent. Kant's example is 'Every alteration has its cause'.

Thus we feel that we are on fairly safe ground when, in the *Foundations*, Kant tells us that

> [it is] of the utmost necessity to construct a pure moral philosophy which is completely freed from everything which may be only empirical and thus belong to anthropology.... A philosophy which mixes pure principles with empirical ones does not deserve the name (*Foundations*, 389–90; Beck, 5–6).

The function of pure moral philosophy, Kant's task in the *Foundations*, is then to deal only with *a priori* connections between concepts *a priori* in origin. It should deal only with principles 'derived from the universal concept of a rational being generally'.

But alas, though Kant's intention is clear, his execution is not. He is so interested (and rightly so) in drawing the distinction between moral principles and empirical generalisations about human behaviour that he forgets to keep his distinction between pure principles and merely *a priori* principles clearly in mind. He thus often refers to any moral principle at all as 'pure' – meaning in this case only that it is not an empirical generalisation. So in a context of supposedly pure

62

moral philosophy, he introduces such 'pure' judgments as 'One ought not make a false promise' and 'One ought not commit suicide'. But in Kant's technical sense of 'pure', the sense in which the *Foundations* is supposed to be an exercise in pure moral philosophy, these judgments are obviously not pure at all. They are indeed *a priori*, for the connection (for example) between making a promise and being obligated to keep it is not merely contingent (since one who recognised no *prima facie* obligation to keep a promise would reveal a failure to understand the concept of promising). However, these judgments are not pure because the concept of making a promise presupposes certain empirical social institutions, and the taking of one's life presupposes the empirically determined concept of being mortal. Thus, as usual, Kant is not keeping his terminology straight.

For this reason, the relationship between the *Metaphysics of Morals* and the work which serves as its *Foundations* is often misperceived. The *Foundations*, as pure moral philosophy, is a work which seeks to analyse the notion of rational action as such. The *Metaphysics of Morals*, using empirical knowledge from anthropology and psychology, seeks to apply the findings of the *Foundations* to man, an imperfectly rational being. Any application of the Categorical Imperative which depends for its application on some empirical fact about man (e.g. that he desires his happiness or has a promising institution) is not a proper part of pure philosophy and has no legitimate place in the *Foundations*. It belongs rather to a metaphysics of morals which '[takes as its object] the particular *nature* of man, which is known only by experience, to show in it the implications of the universal moral principles' (*Metaphysics of Morals*, 216; Gregor, 14).[6]

My concern in this chapter is only with Kant's pure moral philosophy in the technical sense of that term. I shall examine the Categorical Imperative (CI_1) as a pure principle of a fully rational being whose actions 'are objectively necessary without making any reference to a purpose, i.e. without having any other end' (*Foundations*, 415; Beck, 32). We shall find that Kant's view, though complex in expression, is neither obscure nor absurd. It seems absurd only if we take it to be a piece of high-level moral advice and wonder how in the world we could ever apply it. The answer to this is simple: as a pure principle, it cannot be applied *simpliciter*. It is a pure metaethical principle and is not in itself, until supplemented with some facts about human nature, a normative criterion of moral rightness.

So the first interesting thing to note about the Categorical Imperative as CI_1, a pure principle of moral philosophy, is that its imperative form is both irrelevant and misleading. For pure moral philosophy is concerned with *all* rational beings, fully rational ones as well as partially rational ones. But CI_1 is an imperative *only* for a will which is, like the human will, subject to inclination:

> A perfectly good will, therefore, would be equally subject to objective laws (of the good), but it would not be conceived as constrained by them . . ., because, according to its own subjective constitution, it can be determined to act only through the conception of the good. Thus no imperatives hold for the divine will, or more generally, for a holy will. . . . 'Ought' is properly a 'would' that is valid for every rational being provided that reason is practical for him without hindrance (*Foundations*, 413–14, 449; Beck, 30–1, 67).

Thus in expressing CI_1 as an imperative, Kant is again mixing up his pure moral philosophy with the application of that philosophy to a creature like man. The holy will *would* of necessity act only upon that maxim that it could will to be a universal law, but it makes no sense to say that it *ought* so to act. The holy will does necessarily what a human will does only under constraint, and thus it is only with regard to human volition that the categorical demand of morality is properly expressed as an imperative. Thus CI_1 should be expressed *descriptively* in terms of how a fully rational being would act. We might formulate such an expression along something like the following lines: X is a fully rational being if and only if X is a being which acts only on maxims that are universalisable.

Taking this principle out of the imperative mood serves at least one useful purpose. For, once in the indicative, the principle ceases to look quite so much like a piece of high-level moral advice. If the activities of a fully rational being can have any effect on our action as advice at all, it is only as an Ideal of Reason – which requires a model or typic for any useful application to man.

Granted that in his pure moral philosophy Kant is attempting to describe the activity of a fully rational being, that he is not interested in human morality but in the essence of rational morality itself, what are we to make of the details of his description? The fully rational being is one which would always act only on universalisable maxims. But what sense can we give to 'universalisable' that is pure and thus still a part of his metaethical inquiry into the foundations for a metaphysics of morals? To answer this question, it will be necessary to explore in detail the various formulations that Kant gives to CI_1.

Moral Universalisation and Freedom

Almost everyone now agrees that moral judgments must, in some sense, be universalisable. And this agreement is typically taken to be an agreement with a central contribution of Kantian ethics. Much that is currently said about moral universalisation, however, would have been strongly rejected by Kant. And so the label 'universalist' does not of itself aid our understanding of Kant's position at all and can easily interfere with such understanding.

R. M. Hare, for example, offers a theory of moral universalisation that is often regarded as Kantian in character. According to Hare, the fundamental principle of morality is the principle that whatever rule any agent applies to other persons he must also apply, or be willing to have applied, to himself, and conversely. This is, according to Hare, simply the demand that moral judgments must, as a requirement of rationality, be universalisable.[7] This theory is quite clearly formal (i.e. any end or purpose can be a part of morality so long as the agent wills it for everyone including himself), and it does appear initially plausible to say that it enshrines a kind of Kantianism. But this is a misleading impression.

First of all, it is important to see how very strange Hare's view really is. For it is really quite radically subjective in character. For Hare, the universalisability of a judgment depends solely upon what the agent is *willing* to accept. He is not claiming that a universalisable moral judgment is one which in fact could obtain as a universal practice. Rather it is one which the agent does will to accept as a universal practice. No matter how evil or unworkable the state of affairs, if the agent is willing that he and everyone else labour under it, then the judgment is moral. The universalisability of a judgment, then, is not determined by any objective state of affairs in the agent's environment, but only by what the agent is or is not willing to put up with. 'The test of the agent's wishes for himself *qua* recipient would justify rules which impose on their recipients unjust or immoral hardships, including racial discrimination and even genocide.'[8] If Werner is willing to be exterminated if it is discovered that he is a Jew, then Werner's prescriptive judgment 'Exterminate the Jews' counts as moral. Morality, on this view, becomes essentially a private rather than a public enterprise. As H. L. A. Hart remarks:

> To characterise morality ... as *primarily* a matter of the application to conduct of those ultimate principles which the individual accepts or to which he commits himself for the conduct of his life seems to me an excessively Protestant approach. Important as this aspect or kind of moral judgment is, we need to understand it as a development from the primary phenomenon of the morality of a social group.[9]

Now it must be admitted that Kant's statement of

the Categorical Imperative would, if viewed uncritically, incline one to interpret Kant as holding a similar position:

> Act only according to that maxim by which you can at the same time will that it should become a universal law (*Foundations*, 421; Beck, 39).

This certainly sounds as though Kant, like Hare, were saying that you act on moral (as opposed to private) grounds so long as you are simply willing that your maxims be universal. However, we should be suspicious of pinning such a view on Kant, for we must remember that his exercise in pure moral philosophy is to discover the nature of fully rational action. And the imposition of genocide by a fanatic hardly seems to correspond with such an Ideal paradigm of rationality – no matter how much the fanatic is willing to suffer the awful consequences of what he does. And indeed, if we proceed a few paragraphs farther in the *Foundations*, we find that Kant's view is considerably more complex than Hare's:

> We must be able to will that a maxim of our action become a universal law; this is the canon of the moral estimation of our action generally. Some actions are of such a nature that their maxim cannot even be thought as a universal law of nature without contradiction.... In others this internal impossibility is not found, though it is still impossible to *will* that their maxim should be raised to the universality of a law of nature, because such a will would contradict itself (*Foundations*, 424; Beck, 41–2).

So Kant is really operating here with *two* principles of morality. The first, used to derive perfect duties when later employed as a criterion, is that you should act on no maxim which is *incapable* of being a universal practice. The second, later used as a criterion for imperfect duties, is that certain maxims, even if capable of being universal practices, cannot count as moral if the agent cannot *consistently* will that they be universal practices. And neither of these principles is subjective. The first speaks of what is *possible* as a universal law. The second speaks, not just of what can be willed (for, as the existence of irrational people surely shows, anything can be willed), but what can be *consistently* willed. And, as I shall argue later, by 'consistently willable' Kant does not mean merely consistency with whatever contingent desires I, by some personal quirk, just happen to have. Rather he means consistency with the desires that all men necessarily have. These desires he calls 'essential ends of humanity', and they play a crucial role in Kant's material metaphysics of morals.

Kant's views on moral universalisation, then, are not formal in the sense that Hare's are. But what are his views then? To see this, we shall need to examine the three *pure* formulations of the Categorical Imperative. These are all recognisable by the fact that they make no reference to nature or to humanity, but are stated as characteristic of rationality as such. They may all be expressed in the indicative mood, and they should be so expressed to avoid confusion between pure and applied moral philosophy. For my working formulations, I shall use the following:

1. X is a fully rational being if and only if X acts on maxims that are universalisable.
2. X is a fully rational being if and only if X treats rationality, whether in its own being or in that of another, always as an end and never as a means only.
3. X is a fully rational being if and only if X acts as though he were a law-making member in a universal kingdom of ends.[10]

What I wish to argue in the remainder of this chapter is that formulation (2) is the fundamental formulation of the Categorical Imperative. It, and the doctrine of 'ends in themselves' upon which it rests, are absolutely essential to understanding what Kant means by moral universalisation.

Now the deduction of formulation (1) from the concept of a rational being is easily presented. Kant does

68

not actually give us the argument in the *Foundations* (except as an enthymeme), but by adding a premise (*b*) from the *Critique of Pure Reason*, we can get the following:

(*a*) X is a fully rational being if and only if X acts only according to a conception of law (at *Foundations*, 412; Beck, 28).

(*b*) X is a law only if X is universal (at *Critique of Pure Reason*, A 2; Kemp Smith, 42).

Therefore: X is a fully rational being if and only if X acts according to a conception of universal law.

We seem to have, then, as a fundamental principle of a fully rational being, that it acts only on a conception of universal laws. However, having this principle is not in itself any great asset in our inquiry into pure moral philosophy. For, as it stands, the notion of 'universal law' lacks specification and cannot be brought to bear upon specifically moral issues. For surely we would not want to claim, for example, that there is any moral significance in acting on a conception of the law of universal gravitation – though such action certainly satisfies a bare criterion of universalisability.

This difficulty, however, is more apparent than real. For we must remember that we are talking about the universalisability of *maxims* – principles of human action. But behaving in accordance with the law of universal gravitation has no maxim because such behaviour is not, in any meaningful sense, an action at all. For it is not within my power to refrain from behaving in accordance with this law. Though my jumping off a building might very well be an action of mine, we should hardly want to say that my falling and hitting the ground was also an action on my part. It is not something I *did*, but something which happened to me. Thus in spelling out universalisability in any ethically relevant sense (in a sense characterising intentional human actions), we must remember that what must be universalisable is not brute bodily behaviour as such, but the maxims of actions. Universalisability thus cannot be spelled out as simply consistency with actual laws of nature. I act according to these, surely, but not on a *conception* of them.

Neither can 'universalisable' mean 'logical consistency' in any formal sense. We can know whether a given statement is formally consistent without knowing anything about the content of the statement. This is, after all, the value of formal procedures. They test the logical consistency of statements once the actual terms or content of these statements have been replaced by variables. For example, we know that the statement 'All grinches are greeps and there is one grinch which is not a greep' is formally inconsistent without knowing anything at all about the meaning and content of the actual statement. For the general schema 'All Ps are Qs and there is a P which is not a Q' is formally inconsistent, i.e. it is reducible to a contradiction of the form 'P and not P'. But the universalisability of maxims *does* indeed depend upon the content of those maxims. Universalisability is supposed to be a rational criterion of *conduct*, not of statements, and must take account of the *ends* that the agent is pursuing in action. The maxim 'I shall make a false promise' is, according to Kant, not universalisable. But it obviously is not a formal contradiction, nor can it be reduced to one. What is not universalisable in this maxim is not its logical form, but is rather the end or purpose that the agent is seeking to bring about.

My reason for discussing these points has been to show that universalisability cannot in itself stand as a sufficient condition for rational morality. For, if taken as sufficient, the sphere of morally permissible actions will include those that merely accord with natural causal laws (e.g. 'survival of the fittest') and those which can be given a non-contradictory description (e.g. 'kill the Jews'). Thus the notion of universalisability must, if it is to be of any real help at all in determining a characterisation of the moral point of view, be spelled out so as to be explicitly relevant to *maxims* – principles for the realisation of certain ends, purposes or states of affairs. All maxims are of the form 'To bring about so and so under certain conditions', and we need some principle to tell us the difference between what is rational to bring about and what is irrational to bring about. Moral actions must be universalisable or rationally consistent – but consistent with *what*?

Here real difficulties begin to present themselves. We must remember that Kant is trying to present his characterisation of the supreme principle of morality as a part of *pure* moral philosophy. Thus he cannot spell out universalisability in terms of any particular empirical ends or purposes that rational beings just *happen* to have, e.g. happiness. Rather he seeks a characterisation of the actions of all rational beings, and there is no reason to suppose that all rational beings pursue the same material ends. And even if they did, this would still be a contingent matter and could not form the basis for the *a priori* principles of pure moral philosophy. But (and this is a very important 'but') if there were an end actually *set by reason itself*, then the case would be quite different:

> Is it a necessary law for all rational beings that they should always judge their actions by such maxims as they themselves could will to serve as universal laws? If it is such a law, it must be connected (wholly *a priori*) with the concept of the will of a rational being as such. But, in order to discover this connection we must, however reluctantly, take a step into metaphysics.

> Material ends ... are without exception only relative, for only their relation to a particularly constituted faculty of desire in the subject gives them their worth. And this worth cannot, therefore, afford any universal principles for all rational beings.

> But suppose that there were something the existence of which in itself had absolute worth, something which, as an end in itself, could be a ground of definite laws. In it and only in it could lie the ground of a possible categorical imperative, i.e. of a practical law.

Thus if there is to be a supreme practical principle and a categorical imperative for the human will, it must be one that forms an objective principle of the will from the conception of that which is necessarily an end for everyone because it is an end in itself (*Foundations*, 426–9; Beck, 44–7).

These passages are too often overlooked. I quote them at length because they are fundamental to an understanding of what Kant is doing in his presentation of the supreme principle of morality. He says two things in these passages that are very important to notice. First, in the sentence beginning 'If it is such a law ...' and the sentence beginning 'Thus if there is to be a supreme practical principle...', Kant is telling us that, contrary to what is often believed, he has *not* established the form of universalisability (1) as the fundamental principle. *If* there is such a principle, it must be *grounded* in some morally relevant metaphysical fact about the nature of rational beings as such. Universalisability is deducible from the concept of a rational being, but this gives us just a necessary condition for rational morality. It must be something else about rational beings that will provide a full set of necessary and sufficient conditions for morality.

The second interesting thing in these passages is that they tell us what this 'something else' must be. It must be an end of absolute worth set by reason itself. The sphere of moral action that is fully rational can be characterised only by reference to a *value* that is fully rational.

Prima facie, this is all very surprising. For from Kant's polemical passages at *Foundations*, 415 (Beck, 32–3) and elsewhere, we might suppose that ends have no place in determining the nature of rational morality. However, it becomes clear in his discussion at *Foundations*, 427 (Beck, 45) that he previously meant that merely *subjective* ends have no place in determining the nature of rational morality. For merely subjective ends are simply ends that rational beings happen to have or desire. These can at most serve as grounds for hypothetical imperatives of the form 'If you want

X, do *Y*'. *Objective* ends, however, are not ends which rational beings happen to desire as a matter of fact, but are ends which a rational being *must*, in so far as he is rational, desire or (if 'desire' is an inappropriate word) seek to promote. These ends are not only desired but desirable. Kant is thus here in fundamental disagreement with such philosophers as David Hume who claim that reason has no role in the determination of ends but merely serves a calculative function. There are, according to Kant, ends which a fully rational being *must* pursue. And this is possible only if the ends themselves are set by reason.

Now what end or ends are in fact set by pure reason? If we are to define morality in terms of such an end, it must not be subjective but must be an objective end of absolute worth. Kant assumes that there is only one such end and thinks it quite obvious what this end is – namely, *rational nature itself*:

Now, I say, man and, in general, every rational being exists as an end in himself and not merely as a means to be arbitrarily used by this or that will.... Such beings are not merely subjective ends whose existence as a result of our action has a worth for us, but are objective ends, i.e. beings whose existence in itself is an end. Such an end is one for which no other end can be substituted, to which these beings should serve merely as a means. For, without them, nothing of absolute worth could be found, and if all worth is conditional and thus contingent, no supreme practical principle for reason could be found anywhere. Thus if there is to be a supreme principle and a categorical imperative for the human will, it must be one that forms an objective principle of the will from the conception of that which is necessarily an end for everyone because it is an end in itself. Hence this objective principle can serve as a universal practical law. The ground of this principle is: rational nature exists as an end in itself (*Foundations*, 428–9; Beck, 47).

Every rational being is of absolute worth, and it is

73

this fact that provides the touchstone whereby the notion of *moral* universalisability can be understood. To claim that a maxim is universalisable is not just to say that it is logically consistent or is in accord with a law of nature. It is rather to claim the following: that universal action on the basis of this maxim *is consistent with the value as an end in itself of every rational being.* In less Kantian language, the rational being will insure that in pursuing his own ends (whatever they may be) he leaves every other rational being the *freedom* to pursue his own ends. Thus

> [the] principle of humanity and of every rational creature as an end in itself is the supreme limiting condition on the freedom of the actions of each man.... Rational nature is distinguished from others in that it provides an end to itself.... It is what must never be acted against, and which must never be valued merely as a means but in every volition also as an end.... That in the use of means to every end I should restrict my maxim to the condition of its universal validity as a law is tantamount to saying that the subject of ends, the rational being itself, must be made the basis of all maxims and must be treated never as a mere means but as the supreme limiting condition in the use of all means, i.e. as an end at the same time (*Foundations*, 430–8; Beck, 49–56).

To say, as is so often said, that the Categorical Imperative is simply a formal test for consistency or is simply the command 'Do not be biased in your own favour' does not do justice to the complexities of Kant's view. Kant certainly wants to claim that no true morality is biased. But this is not because the essence of morality is to act unbiasedly. Rather it is because biased action in one's own favour is inconsistent with the real essence of morality: the recognition of the absolute worth of each rational being and the controlling of actions accordingly. I am to treat others as ends in themselves because they *are* ends in themselves. That is, I treat other rational beings as ends in themselves by respect-

74

ing in them that same value which I find and seek to defend in myself – freedom.[11]

What Kant gives us, then, is a moral equivalent of a Leibnizian Principle of Sufficient Reason. Rationality draws no distinctions between qualitative identicals, and thus there can be no rational ground for giving moral preference to one rational being (e.g. myself) over another. And this is where *moral* universalisation makes its entrance. To ask if my maxim or plan is morally universalisable is not to inquire merely into its logical or causal possibility. Rather it is to inquire if the maxim, if realised in action, would either directly or indirectly involve treatment of any other rational being as a mere means rather than as an end in itself. Such treatment would be direct if, for example, it involved an aggressive invasion against the freedom of another. It would be indirect if the action in question would not be compatible with all other rational beings acting in this way in similar circumstances. I may reveal a disrespect for rational beings, not merely by exploiting them directly, but also by claiming for myself a liberty in action which is not compatible with a like liberty for all.

Morality thus has to be characterised in terms of the end in itself – the rational being. The value of this objective or rational end provides the object which must not be acted against in any proposed code of conduct that could count as a rational morality. Formulation (2) is thus revealed as the fundamental formulation of the Categorical Imperative – the formulation which provides the value or end in terms of which morality must be defined.[12]

We have thus realised the goal of our inquiry in this chapter: a discovery of the necessary and sufficient conditions for a rational morality. I submit the following as an interpretation of Kant's position in this regard:

For any code of conduct C, C is a system of rational morality (or is a real moral system) if and only if the maxims of the actions prescribed in C are such that their universal performance would leave secured the

75

value of each rational being as an end in itself having absolute worth, i.e. would leave each rational being free to pursue his own ends in action.

Now is this a formal characterisation? In Kant's sense of 'formal' it certainly is. For morality is not characterised by reference to any particular material or subjective end that rational beings just happen to have. However, Kant's characterisation is certainly not formalistic in the sense previously outlined. This sense of formalism, it will be remembered, was the following: A metaethical characterisation of the moral point of view is formalistic if it defines morality without reference to any value, end or purpose that provides the content of morality. If a philosopher believed that morality could be defined (for example) solely in terms of logical consistency, he would be a metaethical formalist in this sense. But Kant does not think that the sphere of morality can be characterised independently of *all* ends, only of all material and subjective ends. Morality must be characterised in terms of the value of each rational being, i.e. in terms of a specified objective end. As an end of pure reason, this is certainly a very special kind of end. But an end it is none the less.

Now at this point I can foresee two possible objections to the interpretation of Kant that I have been presenting. I shall now develop these objections and attempt to answer them.

Objection (*a*): How can it be claimed that morality is grounded upon the value of each rational being as an end when Kant explicitly tells us in the *Critique of Practical Reason* (57–66; Beck, 59–68) that good and evil ends cannot be defined prior to the moral law?

It will be useful to counter this objection in two ways. The first way consists in pointing out that no claim has been made that the value of rational nature is *moral* value. I have claimed (as an interpretation of

76

Kant) that each rational being is an end in itself of absolute worth, but I have not claimed that the rational being is a *moral* end or is of absolute *moral* worth. Thus to show that the moral law cannot be defined in terms of moral good is not to show that it cannot be defined in terms of some non-moral good or end. Since I shall develop this reply in detail in dealing with the second objection, I shall not say any more about it at this point. Rather I shall concentrate upon a second and more general criticism implicit in this passage from the second *Critique*. For one might interpret this passage as a claim that *no* end (moral or otherwise) could provide a definition of the moral law.

The chief confusion in this passage from the second *Critique* lies in Kant's ambiguous use of the term 'ground' (*Grund*). For this term is used by Kant to mean either of two very different concepts. Often, the 'ground of morality' means simply that which *motivates* us to perform a moral action (ground$_1$). At other times, the term 'ground' refers to those rational ends in terms of which we may *define* the moral law as an objective statement (ground$_2$). Keeping this distinction in mind, we can see more clearly what is going on in the passage in question.

Kant does indeed tell us that no end can ground$_2$ a definition of morality. However, his reasons for saying this reveal that what he means is that no merely *subjective* end can ground$_2$ morality. Subjective ends could justify only hypothetical imperatives, and a creature which acted only on hypothetical imperatives would not be an autonomous rational being. For his motives in acting would necessarily spring only from phenomenal sensuous inclination. Objective ends, however, are *worthy* of rational desire even if, in fact, they are not desired by partially rational creatures (e.g. man). Thus a morality justified in terms of objective ends would not be a heteronomous morality, for the origin of the ends would lie in reason rather than in sensuous inclination.

Kant's lack of clarity in making this simple point results from his not keeping the following two questions distinct:

1. What, objectively, ought to be done?
2. Why would a fully rational being do what ought to be done?

When we say that an end of intrinsic worth grounds$_2$ rational morality, we mean that it determines the general outlines of what could count as an objectively right or obligatory action. We do *not* mean that such an end grounds$_1$ morality; that is, we do not mean that *desire* for this end, even if it is of absolute worth, determines the will of the rational agent. The fully rational agent's motive in doing what he ought is simply his recognition that he ought, not his desire for the end of the action. Thus what the passage really argues is that the motive for morality must not be the desire for a particular end, i.e. that morality must not be grounded$_1$ in any end. But this does not show that morality cannot be grounded$_2$ in an end, i.e. cannot be defined in terms of an objective end. In presenting an objective characterisation of morality, we are employed in a theoretical and not a practical task. Thus the question of possible heteronomy does not even arise so long as merely subjective ends are kept out of the picture.

Objection (*b*): Kant's argument, as you present it, is circular. For you claim that we cannot understand his characterisation of morality except in terms of his doctrine that rational beings have worth as ends in themselves. But is not the value or worth of rational nature itself a *moral* value? Is not the reason that a rational being has worth at all simply that he possesses a morally good will? If so, then Kant is defining morality in terms of a moral value, and this is obviously circular.

Now it seems to me that this objection, as stated, is by no means conclusive against Kant. Unfortunately, however, there is a more subtle version of this objection which is conclusive. Thus, in the last analysis, it will be necessary to patch up Kant's view in order to show how it can be saved from the charge of circularity. But before doing this, I shall first show why the stated objection does not work.

It is commonly assumed among Kant commentators that Kant believes that the value of the rational being as an end depends upon the possession by that being of a good or moral will. Some go so far as to claim that rational nature and the good will are identical. H. J. Paton, for example, claims the following:

> An end in itself must ... be a self-existent end, not something to be produced by us. Since it has absolute worth, we know already what it must be – namely, a good will. This good or rational will Kant takes to be present in every rational agent, and so in every man, however much it may be overlaid by irrationality.[13]

If this is Kant's view, it has some unpleasant consequences. Not only does it render his characterisation of morality circular, but it also renders Kant's doctrine perverse on the practical level. For the second formulation of the Categorical Imperative would reduce to the following: Treat all persons possessing a good will as ends and never as means only. But surely this will not do. For Kant tells us again and again that we can never know if another person has in fact a good will, a good will being an unobservable and non-inferable noumenal disposition. Thus we would never be morally bound to treat another as an end, because we could never know if the person was *worth* being treated as an end. It is, of course, true that all fully rational beings have good wills. But the second formulation claims that *all* rational beings deserve to be treated as ends, not just fully rational ones. And it is by no means true that all rational beings have good wills. Paton's contention that the good will is present 'in every man' is, according to Kant, just not so. If it were so, the whole point of making imperative moral judgments would be lost.[14] Thus the value of the rational being as an end cannot really depend upon that being's possession of a good will.

Now this is by no means inconsistent with Kant's

79

claim that the only thing good in itself is a good will. For it may well be that the rational being is an end in itself, and has absolute worth, without being *morally* good in itself at all. Thus, though the good will may be the only thing morally good in itself, it may not be the only thing which is an end in itself of absolute worth. Whether or not this is so depends upon whether Paton is correct in assuming that at *Foundations*, 428 (Beck, 46) we 'know already' what the objective end of morality must be from the previous discussion of the good will at *Foundations*, 393 (Beck, 9). For it may be that Paton has overlooked the possibility that, in speaking of the rational will as an end in itself, Kant is introducing a *new* value.

In fact, this is precisely what Kant is doing. For he does not say that the value of the rational being depends upon its possession of a good will or, in less Kantian terms, upon its being morally virtuous. What he does say is that the value of the rational being derives, not from its morality, but from that which renders it capable of being moral at all, i.e. it derives from its *freedom*. The value that this gives to a rational being Kant calls its 'dignity'.

> That which constitutes the condition under which alone something can be an end in itself does not have mere relative worth, i.e. a price, but an intrinsic worth, i.e. *dignity*. Now morality is the condition under which alone a rational being can be an end in itself, because only through it is it possible to be a legislative member in the realm of ends. Thus morality and humanity, in so far as it is capable of morality, alone have dignity (*Foundations*, 435; Beck, 53).

The worth of a rational being, and thus the worth of man, consists therefore in his autonomy from the course of mere phenomenal nature. For his dignity consists in his being a self-legislative member in a realm of ends. Thus it seems that the dreaded circle is avoided. For to say that a being is of worth because it is free and capable of being moral is not thereby to make a moral judgment about the being. Indeed, 'dignity' can hardly be a term of moral evaluation, for it is predicated of morality itself.

But, alas, this avoidance of circularity is only apparent. It must be remembered that we are attempting to *define* morality. And if we are to give it a non-circular definition in terms of some value like freedom, we must be able to understand the meaning of 'freedom' ('self-legislation') without having to appeal to any moral notions. This, unfortunately, is just what Kant's doctrine of freedom will not let us do. For freedom is for him a morally loaded notion, and thus an inescapable circularity results in his characterisation of morality itself. Consider some of the things he says in the *Metaphysics of Morals* about freedom and the dignity it confers on man:

> Some have tried to define freedom of choice as the power to choose between the alternatives of acting with or against the law. But freedom of choice cannot be defined in this way, although the power of choice as *phenomenon* gives us frequent examples of this in experience. For we know freedom (as it is first made knowable to us through the moral law) only as a *negative* property in us: the property of not being *necessitated* to act by any sensuous determining ground.

> The positive concept of freedom is that of the power of pure reason to be of itself practical.

> Man regarded as a *person* – that is, as the subject of morally practical reason – is exalted above any price. . . . When, as he must do, he regards himself not merely as a person as such but also as a man – that is, as a person who has duties laid upon him by his own reason – his insignificance as a *natural man* cannot detract from his consciousness of his dignity as a *moral* man (225, 212–13, 433–4; Gregor, 25, 10, 99).

What Kant seems to be arguing in these passages is

that a will which is *really* free is a will which must act in accordance with a practical law of reason, i.e. must act morally. An immoral act of will is not really a free act of will, at least not in the fully positive sense of 'free'. Thus we cannot really know what it means to act freely unless we understand what it is to act morally. Morality is the *ratio cognoscendi* of freedom (*Critique of Practical Reason*, 4; Beck, 4). In the passage at *Foundations*, 435 (Beck, 53) where he says that man's dignity results from his capacity to be moral, it seems that he means just this and nothing more (not, for example, his capacity of choosing to do evil also). Man's value as an end lies in the fact that he is potentially, if not actually, a moral being. The circle thus still faces us.

Now there seems to me only one way to patch up Kant's doctrine so that his characterisation of morality will not be circular. And this is to develop the concept of freedom in such a way that it will not have a value that is necessarily moral or which necessarily depends upon some moral value. And this is at least a *prima facie* plausible move. For moral value is usually ascribed to persons, motives and actions – not to objects or states of being. We value such things as happiness and freedom, but it is odd to say that these things have a moral value – even if morality is defined as the pursuit of these objects.[15] Thus it will be useful to forage around in Kant's text to see if there is any evidence at all for reinterpreting his final conclusion about the value of freedom. Fortunately, there is such evidence.

Kant uses the phrase 'free will' or simply 'freedom' quite ambiguously. Though he has two technical meanings of freewill, he usually fails to keep them separate. His technical uses are as follows:

Free *Willkür*: Freedom of choice or the spontaneous self-activity of persons.

Free *Wille*: Autonomy or acting on the basis of a universal moral law of reason.[16]

The issue that faces us thus becomes clear. If the

value of a rational being depends upon his possessing a free *Wille*, then Kant's characterisation of morality is indeed circular. And the passages quoted above seem to indicate that this is the sense of freedom which he has in mind. However, if we can make a case that it is free *Willkür*, and not free *Wille*, which confers dignity upon man, then we shall have saved Kant's characterisation of morality from circularity. For then man's dignity would not derive from his capacity to be moral, but from his self-legislative capacity to choose *any* course of action – his freedom to choose his course of action (be it moral, immoral, or non-moral) rather than having it forced upon him by sensuous inclination. This seems at least a plausible view. For it simply is not true that the evil man is always one who is overcome by sensuous inclination. He could be one who acts upon an evil maxim which, though evil, was still pure and did not have its motivational appeal in the matter of sensuous inclination. The man who makes it his maxim to act in a thoroughly Satanic fashion (to do evil because it is evil) would be a case in point. It is an old theological doctrine that man's high place upon the Great Chain of Being derives from his power to be either virtuous or sinful. And this seems a more sensible view than that which would locate man's dignity in a necessity to act morally. (This latter view of freedom has, with considerable justice, been satirised by Bertrand Russell as 'freedom to obey the police'.)

Though Kant of course does not himself draw this conclusion, his text seems to me to contain sufficient material whereby this conclusion may be drawn. Thus, as an argument to show that man's dignity derives from his possessing free *Willkür* (not free *Wille*),[17] I propose the following:

(a) That which gives man his dignity is that which essentially distinguishes him from brutes and physical objects (at *Metaphysics of Morals*, 222, 385, 434–5; Gregor, 22, 45, 99–100).
(b) That which essentially distinguishes man from brutes and physical objects (makes him a person instead of a thing) is that he is responsible or

83

accountable for what he does, i.e. that his actions can be imputed to him (at *Metaphysics of Morals*, 222; Gregor, 22).

(c) The necessary and sufficient condition for holding a man accountable is that he have a free *Willkür* (at *Religion*, 21–5; Greene and Hudson, 17–21; and *Critique of Practical Reason*, 100; Beck, 103).

Therefore: That which gives a man his dignity is his possession of a free *Willkür*.

The only premise of this argument which is at all controversial as an interpretation is (c). From some passages I have quoted earlier, it might seem that Kant wants to make a stronger claim – namely, that free *Wille* is demanded before we can legitimately hold a man responsible.[18] However, there are other passages where this is explicitly denied. The wisdom lies with these latter passages. For if we take free *Wille* as necessary for accountability, we find that Kant is involved in something very like the Socratic paradox at the level of freedom. Intentional wrongdoing would be an indication that freedom was lacking. But note the perverse consequence of this view if taken seriously: We could not legitimately hold a person responsible for an intentional wrong action! For commission of such an action would in itself be sufficient excuse to absolve the agent from any blame. This is an absurd consequence, and it is a consequence which Kant himself does not embrace. But he fails to realise that this consequence follows from demanding free *Wille*, and not simply free *Willkür*, as the necessary and sufficient condition for accountability. Also, to treat another as an end in himself is at a minimum to recognise him as a source of claims. As such a source, he deserves respect even if his claims and actions are in our judgment immoral. His demands may be overridden, but they cannot be simply ignored. Bad men are still men; they are not animals or things.[19] Thus it seems to me imperative on several counts that we adopt free *Willkür*, and not free *Wille*, as that which gives man his dignity. This not only saves Kant's characterisation of morality from circularity, but also keeps his doctrine from being perverse on the practical level.

We have, then, on this modification, a non-circular definition of morality. Kant is to be taken as defining morality in terms of the non-moral value of each free (free *Willkür*) rational agent. To define morality in terms of some value which is not moral is not as odd as it might at first appear. For probably no utilitarian takes happiness to be a moral value, though each believes that morality is to be defined in terms of this value. Similarly with such values as pleasure, self-realisation, tranquillity and contemplation. These are all values in terms of which morality has been defined, yet none of these things (because they are not motives, actions or persons) can properly be said to have moral value.

Thus we treat rational beings as ends because of their freedom of *Willkür*, because they are responsible persons and not things. This freedom to choose for good or evil is what gives morality a point. For if man were not capable of choosing to better himself, then it would be pointless to address imperatives of rational morality to him. One might as well talk morality to stones or dogs. Similarly, if man could only do good, such imperatives would also be pointless. One might then as well talk morality to God or angels. Freedom of *Willkür* is thus the *ratio essendi* of morality – the condition without which it would be pointless.

In summary, it will be useful to employ Paton's distinction between the *essence* of morality and the *criterion* of morality. The essence of morality is simply a definition or set of necessary and sufficient conditions for what counts as morality. The essence of morality, for Kant, is simply action that honours the absolute worth of all rational beings by respecting their freedom. The essence of morality is thus not formalistic.

Now the essence of morality is not, as it stands, an adequate moral criterion. It does not tell us how, in particular cases, we are to determine the rightness or wrongness of particular courses of action. To know that we should treat all rational beings as ends in themselves is not to know a great deal. For what *counts* as treating another as an end? To know this we have to know something about the actual material ends and purposes that human beings have. For what we want to know now is not simply what in general counts as rational action for any rational being, but rather what counts as rational action for humanity. In the following chapter I shall spell out Kant's solution to this problem.

3 The Criterion of Moral Right

Introduction

The essence of morality is revealed in maxims which respect the value as an end in itself of each rational being, i.e. maxims which would, if acted on, leave each rational being free to pursue his own ends in acting. This seems to me the only way to understand Kant's notion of *moral* universalisation.

To have discovered the essence of moral action, however, is not yet to have discovered the *criterion* whereby the moral rightness of human actions may be determined. It is Kant's firm conviction that practical laws are in some sense determined by the Categorical Imperative (which defines the essence of morality), but the details of such determination are far from clear. Practical laws tell us the general kinds of conduct that are permissible and impermissible from the moral point of view. But the only practical law that seems directly derivable from the Categorical Imperative is the following: One ought never to interfere with the freedom of any rational being. On the basis of this practical law, then, we could provide a general characterisation of right action:

X is a right action if and only if the maxim of X, if realised as a universal practice, would not interfere with the freedom of any rational being.

Now it is true that this statement does provide Kant's fundamental characterisation of moral rightness. Kant exalts the sovereignty and integrity of each rational being above all other values. However, if used as a moral criterion for mankind, this principle expresses a naïve optimism. For morality, as defined thus

87

far, is a description of the activity of a fully free, fully rational noumenal being in a community of peers – an Ideal of Pure Reason. To provide a criterion for moral rightness among men, however, some attention must be paid to the obvious fact that man is not a fully free, fully rational being, but a being whose freedom and rationality are finite. The limitations of man cannot, of course, be allowed to change the essence of morality. But these limitations must be considered if we are to determine the degree to which moral notions can apply to man at all.

It is easy to see why this is so. In dealing with fully rational noumenal beings, we may be confident that each of them will not pursue ends or purposes which would interfere with the freedom of their fellows. There would be no conflict of interest in a community of fully rational beings, each having a holy will. But in dealing with human beings, such a community is only an Ideal. For in fact, human ends and purposes are in constant conflict. Thus if the essence of morality is ever to provide a criterion for human action, it must be such that it can make the best of what is admittedly not an ideal situation. The criterion for a right action that applies to a fully rational being would, if used directly as a criterion for man, generate a kind of moral *laissez-faire* that would shock the conscience of even the most hardened cynic. I could, for example, justify refusal to prevent a rape on the grounds that interference would violate the freedom of another rational being to pursue his own purposes. If it be argued that, by pursuing such a purpose the rapist would be relinquishing his right to treatment as a rational being, I would disagree. The commission of a rape could very well be a manifestation of that which gives man dignity, i.e. a free *Willkür*. Rapists are persons, even if not very nice persons. They are neither animals nor machines.

What we need, obviously, is some way to bring the ideal of pure morality to bear on the concrete empirical contingencies of the human situation. For what is finally rational to do surely depends, at least in part, on the sort of creatures we are. To attack a man with a weapon is clearly to interfere with his freedom in a morally relevant way. If people were differently constituted, however, this might not be the case:

> The common requirements of law and morality consist for the most part not of active services to be rendered but of forbearances, which are usually formulated in negative form as prohibitions. Of these the most important for social life are those that restrict the use of violence in killing or inflicting bodily harm.... Yet ... things might have been, and might one day be, otherwise. There are species of animals whose physical structure (including exoskeletons or a carapace) renders them virtually immune from attack by other members of their species.... If men were to lose their vulnerability to each other there would vanish one obvious reason for the most characteristic provision of law and morals: *Thou shalt not kill.*[1]

Now Kant is by no means insensitive to the problems involved in attempting to apply the pure formulations of the Categorical Imperative. In attempting to meet these problems, he provides three subsidiary formulae of the Categorical Imperative (CI_2) which can, by bringing the moral law 'closer to intuition', provide criteria for moral rightness. The *Foundations*' formulae may be represented as follows:

1. Act only according to that maxim by which you can at the same time will that it should become a universal law of nature.
2. So act as to use humanity, both in your own person and in the person of every other, always at the same time as an end, never simply as a means.
3. All maxims which spring from your own making of laws ought to accord with a possible kingdom of ends as a kingdom of nature (see *Foundations*, 436; Beck, 54–5).

What is central in these formulations is that they

make *nature* the model (Kant's technical term is *typic*) whereby the pure Categorical Imperative is to be applied, and man, a natural creature, the value in terms of which moral universalisation is to be spelled out.[2] Indeed, in the *Metaphysics of Morals* Kant goes so far as to make the old Stoic maxim 'Live according to nature' the basic criterion of moral right. Kant does not, of course, mean to say that being in accord with a possible law of nature is itself a right-making characteristic. The only right-making characteristic is universalisability in terms of rational beings. However, it is Kant's conviction that for human beings moral universalisation can be applied only through the notion of law of nature as a model. When contemplating the morality of any proposed course of action, then, we must ask ourselves two questions: (1) 'Could a system of nature obtain in which such actions were universally practised?' and (2) 'Could I, as a rational being, assent to membership in such a system even if it is possible?' If the answer to both is yes, the action is right. If the answer to either is no, the action is at least *prima facie* wrong.[3]

The Law of Nature

To make any sense at all out of Kant's view that law in nature is the model or typic for the moral law, we must realise that Kant has two distinct conceptions of law in nature. The first of these, the notion of *causal* law, is only indirectly relevant to morality. A causal law simply links phenomena in nature according to a rule of succession. And causal possibility, though a necessary condition for moral possibility, is hardly a sufficient condition. Thus when asking whether or not a given maxim could provide a universal law of nature, we must mean something more than a causal law of nature. A system of nature governed by the maxim 'survival of the fittest' not only could, but does in fact, obtain. This is the law which rules in the animal kingdom. However, though such action meets the condition that it is causally possible, Kant would hardly want to say that (for humans) it is morally permissible. Thus Kant must have in mind some other notion of law in nature to use in forming a moral criterion for rightness.

This other notion is to be found in his doctrine of *teleological* law in nature. The doctrine of teleological law is worked out primarily in the second part of the *Critique of Judgment*. The arguments in this work are so complex that an exposition of them in any detail would take us far afield of our present purpose. For our present inquiry, it will be sufficient merely to summarise some of the leading conclusions contained in Kant's discussion.

In the third *Critique*, Kant develops his notion of the final end of creation. This end provides the goal of nature as a self-unfolding teleological process. Kant does not, of course, teach that nature is in fact such a process. Such a position would be manifestly inconsistent with the leading doctrines of the first *Critique*. However, it is a useful fiction in science, morality and aesthetics if we view the universe *as if* it were a goal-directed process.

Now since there is only one thing which qualifies as an end in itself (the rational being), Kant believes that the final end of nature must be man – the only rational being who is also natural:

> What is the end and purpose of these and all the preceding natural kingdoms? For man, we say, and the multifarious uses to which his intelligence teaches him to put all these forms of life. He is the ultimate end of creation here on earth, because he is the only being upon it that is able to form a conception of ends, and from an aggregate of things purposively fashioned to construct by the aid of his reason a system of ends.... All the manifold forms of life ... and even the entire complex that embraces their numerous systems, incorrectly called worlds, would all exist for nothing, if man, or rational beings of some sort, were not to be found in their midst. Without man, in other words, the whole of creation would be a mere wilderness, a thing in

91

vain, and have no final end (*Critique of Judgment*, 426–7, 442; Meredith, 88, 108).

The notion of law in nature which is of interest to morality, then, is law conceived as a process which furthers man as a final end of nature. Causal laws, Kant is quick to admit, obviously do not always operate in such a way that man profits from them. Man is heir to a great many natural disasters, and thus the notion of causal law could hardly provide a model for morality. For it is quite possible for causal laws to operate in such a way as to produce chaos in the world of men. A respect for persons is certainly not revealed by earthquakes, plagues and famines – all phenomena which operate according to causal law. Thus, in finding a model for the moral law in nature, we must look elsewhere than to causal laws.

Teleological laws in nature, in contrast to causal laws, describe phenomenal actions only in so far as these actions promote (or at least do not interfere with) man as the final end of nature. Phenomenal actions are instances of teleological law in so far as they contribute to a systematic harmony of purposes among men. For contributing to such a harmony of purposes is in fact the only way that men can be treated as the final ends of nature. To treat a man as an end is simply to recognise his right to pursue the ends or purposes that he has and to judge conduct right or wrong in so far as it leaves secured or interferes with the maximum realisation of these purposes by each man :

Man is the *ultimate end* of nature, and the one in relation to whom all other natural things constitute a system of ends. What now is the end in man, and the end which, as such, is intended to be promoted by means of his connection with nature? If this end is to be something which must be found in man himself, it must either be of such a kind that man himself may be satisfied by means of nature and its beneficence, or else it is the aptitude and skill for all manner of ends for which he may employ nature both external and internal. The former end of nature would be the *happiness* of man, the latter his *culture* (*Critique of Judgment*, 429–30; Meredith, 92).

To treat a man as an end, then, is simply to recognise his right to pursue his own ends or purposes in action – among these ends happiness and culture. Our typic or model for applying the moral law to man thus amounts to this: Act only on that maxim which could be a universal law of nature. What this means is not that the maxim could be a causal law only, for many things are causally possible that are not morally possible. Rather it means that we should act only on maxims which, if they were causal laws, would be teleological laws also, i.e. would leave secured a systematic harmony of purposes among men:

> Actions which can and ought to be willed in obedience to the moral law ... are those whose maxims, if conceived as a law of nature, would further the systematic harmony of purposes among men, or at least would do nothing to destroy such a systematic harmony.[4]

When Kant speaks of harmony here, he does not mean uniformity. His ideal moral world is not one in which everyone would have the *same* purposes. Rather his view is that the ideal moral world would be one in which each man would have the liberty to realise *all* of his purposes in so far as these purposes are compatible with like liberty for all.

Thus far, then, we are able to conclude this much: The reasonable, the rational and the moral action for man is that action which does not interfere with the systematic harmony of purposes among men. This is a start towards a moral criterion, but it is not a complete criterion as yet. For we still need some moral basis for handling cases of *conflict* between ends or purposes. It is an obvious, if not a very pleasant, fact about men that they often have many purposes whose realisation would thwart the purposes of others. It is due to their pursuit of such purposes that criminals are often described as anti-social beings. Thus, to develop a complete criterion of right action, we must develop a general doctrine as to which purposes are essential to man and thus overriding of other purposes in cases of conflict.

The Essential Ends of Humanity

Kant's first modification of the pure moral law to handle cases of conflict occurs in his *Rechtslehre* (*Metaphysical Elements of Justice*). In applying the moral law directly were attempted, we should be compelled to leave each man free to pursue his own ends – whatever they might be. This, however, would leave us stuck with the rapist example mentioned previously and would hardly produce anything plausibly describable as moral harmony. Fortunately, Kant is wise enough to see that men, being the kind of creatures they are, do not fall under this pure law directly. For it would be a strange kind of valuing of freedom that valued even the freedom to repress freedom. Thus we need some moral basis for interfering with the freedom of those who would use their freedom to deprive others of their rights as men.

Kant provides this basis in his doctrine of the *moral title* or *authorisation* (*Befugnis*).[5] Law, he claims, contains analytically the notion of authority to compel. If Jones's actions are right (i.e. consistent with the freedom of other men), then any action to interfere with him is wrong. If, however, his actions are wrong (i.e. interfere with the freedom of others), then there is a moral title or authority to prevent what he is doing. Kant's justification for saying this is his view that one way to value freedom is to remove obstacles to freedom. Action against the rapist is 'an obstacle to an obstacle' to freedom and is therefore right. There is a moral title to do anything which removes obstacles to freedom. Thus, in applying the characterisation of right to men, we must modify it in the following way:

X is a right action if and only if its maxim would, if

a universal law, allow every rational being to pursue his own ends in action *so long as these ends do not include the denial of freedom to others.*

This condition would be unnecessary for fully rational beings, but for finitely rational beings like man it is absolutely essential. It is this condition which ultimately provides the moral justification for coercive authority by the State:

The formal condition under which nature can alone attain its real end is the existence of a constitution so regulating the mutual relations of men that the abuse of freedom by individuals striving one against another is opposed by lawful authority centred in a whole, called a *civil community* (*Critique of Judgment*, 432; Meredith, 96).

Now all this is sound morality, no doubt, but it is not completely without its problems within the Kantian framework. For though we may applaud this notion of the moral title, we may also wonder where are the premises in the Kantian moral system whereby it can be derived. Kant makes no attempt to derive it from the Categorical Imperative. It is hard to see why he does not do this, since it would seem that the derivation would proceed quite easily. Could the maxim 'Permit the abuse of freedom' be a universal law? Is it morally universalisable? So contrary to a systematic harmony of purposes among men, it surely is not. As a finite rational creature, I necessarily desire that others do not interfere with my freedom. Thus I could not consistently will that a complete moral *laissez-faire* obtain. For I would want others to come to my aid in the event of someone attempting to deprive me of my rights as a man. I could not will this maxim to be a universal law.[6] But not only could I not will it a universal law, it could not *be* a universal law that would secure a harmony of human purpose. For without this rider of the moral title, one would have no security whatever and would exist in a moral chaos very like that described by Hobbes. It would seem, therefore, that there is both an imperfect and a perfect duty to oppose abuses of freedom:

> The compulsion accompanying juridical laws is in no way a hindrance to freedom: on the contrary, it is the necessary condition of outer freedom. In a state of 'lawless freedom', a state of nature characterised by absence of the State's overriding authority, my ability to express my freedom outwardly would be a matter of chance. It would depend upon a merely contingent harmony of my act of choice with that of my neighbour. In such a state, freedom would be essentially 'in collision with itself', since there would be no principle to guarantee that my attempts to express my freedom outwardly will not be checked at every point by others' actions. The freedom of imperfectly rational beings can be only a freedom under laws accompanied by constraint.[7]

Kant's own reason for not attempting a derivation of this limit to freedom from the Categorical Imperative seems to be his belief, already mentioned, that authority to compel is contained in the very concept of law. But this is not completely clear. Though it is true that *positive* law is not logically possible without authority to compel, it is not obvious that this is true of moral law. (And it is moral law that is primarily under discussion at this stage of the argument, for it is moral law that will ultimately have to provide the justification for setting up a system of coercive State law.) Kant's best case for an analytic connection between moral law and compulsion could be made if the discussion was limited to the sphere of moral *rights*. For it does seem odd (even if not analytically false) to say that Jones has a right if it is the case that all other people may ignore that right with impunity. At any rate, the rider of the moral title does seem closely connected to the meaning of 'valuing freedom'. For one makes mockery of the value of toleration if one includes active intolerance among those things we ought to tolerate. We would doubt the sincerity of a man's claim to value freedom if he did not seek to protect it when threatened. .

Thus, whatever we may think of Kant's attempt to demonstrate it, the rider of the moral title is adhered to by Kant and it does seem to make good moral sense. However, even here, we are not through with our problems in attempting to state a criterion for the morally right. For originally our criterion was too broad; it let in as right such actions as ignoring a rape.[8] However, it now seems in danger of being too narrow. It might seem that now we are justified in prohibiting all types of actions of which people disapprove on the grounds that the performing of an action of which others disapprove is to interfere with their freedom. Given a certain interpretation of 'so long as these ends do not include the denial of freedom to others', we have the possibility of a very repressive morality indeed.

Consider, for example, the case of a man who practises homosexual activities, in private, with a consenting adult partner. Are we morally justified in attempting to prohibit his action? An argument to establish that we are so justified might proceed as follows: Such activities cause shock and disgust to those citizens who are aware that they go on – even in private. The average person has, among his ends, the desire to avoid disgust. Thus we are justified in prohibiting private homosexual activities because such activities interfere with the freedom of others to pursue their ends.

Now this is not a very happy sort of argument, and I do not think that Kant would want to be stuck with sanctioning it. He is, on the contrary, very sensitive to such problems. For though he cautions against scandal, he realises that there are many actions which, because of the ignorance and prejudice of others, will have the same emotive effect as scandal without being morally blameworthy. And even if an action fails to measure up to some ideal standard of moral excellence, it will not for that reason alone constitute a breach of moral duty:

> The bad example which one free person affords another as a *scandalum acceptum* is not an infringement of his rights (*Perpetual Peace*, 346; Beck, 89).[9]

What we need, then, is some grading of human ends and purposes on a hierarchy of value so that we may determine which, in cases of conflict, are to override.

Kant attempts to provide a start towards such a grading in his doctrine of the 'essential ends of humanity'. This doctrine is difficult and often muddled; but since it is a great aid to a full understanding of his philosophy of moral right, it will be useful to examine it here in some detail.

As early as the pre-critical *Lectures on Ethics*, Kant is constantly giving a moral criterion which, for a supposed formalist, is strange indeed. Consider the following passages:

> We must have rules to give our actions universal validity and to mould them into a general harmony. These rules are derived from the universal ends of mankind, and they are the moral rules.

> The fundamental rule, in terms of which I ought to restrain my freedom, is the conformity of free behaviour to the essential ends of humanity. I shall not then follow inclinations, but shall bring them under a rule. He who subjects his person to his inclinations acts contrary to the essential end of humanity; for as a free being he must not be subjected to inclinations, but ought to determine them in the exercise of his freedom; and being a free agent he must have a rule, which is the essential end of humanity.

> The conditions under which alone the fullest use of freedom is possible, and can be in harmony with itself, are the essential ends of humanity. It must conform with these. The principle of all duties is that the use of freedom must be in keeping with the essential ends of humanity (pp. 17, 122, 124).

The thing that is odd about Kant's discussion in the *Lectures* is that, though he is constantly telling us that right action is in some way governed by these essential ends, he never tells us just *what* they are and exactly

98

how they do govern moral rightness. The closest he ever comes to identifying the ends is when he tells us that 'man has by nature two impulses, to be esteemed and to be loved' (p. 185). This, however, is not a great deal of help. We already know, of course, that freedom is the supreme limiting condition upon the morality of actions. Thus it is plausible to suppose that freedom will function as an essential end. But we have already seen that freedom alone will not get us out of great difficulties in trying to find in Kant's ethics a viable criterion of moral right.

Now finally, in the third *Critique* and in the *Metaphysics of Morals*, Kant shares with his reader the ends which he takes to be essential to humanity. In the third *Critique*, he claims that man's essential ends are *happiness* and *culture* (429–30; Meredith, 92). And in the *Metaphysics of Morals*, he claims that they are *happiness* and *perfection* (384; Gregor, 44). From what he says in the third *Critique*, it can be seen that what he means by 'culture' there is not essentially different from what he means by 'perfection' in the *Metaphysics of Morals*: the maximum cultivation of one's natural and moral powers and capabilities. Thus I shall work with happiness and perfection as those ends which, on Kant's considered opinion, are essential to humanity.[10]

What is most disturbing and odd is that Kant constantly reiterates the importance of these ends, proceeds confident that he has established their essentiality, but never actually attempts to derive or justify them. Suddenly, there they are; and it seems as though the reader is supposed to take them or leave them, no questions asked. One commentator has found this most disturbing:

> When Kant finally gets down to cases and mentions the obligatory ends that pure practical reason prescribes, he reveals the inadequacy of his argument. Quite like a conjurer pulling rabbits from a hat, he holds up his moral law, turns it over, and taps it to show that it is devoid of content, and then proceeds to pull great fat ends from it with effortless ease.... The details are brilliantly complex, as we would ex-

99

pect from Kant. But the whole has the air of one of those meticulous stories of space travel, complete in every detail, which begin, 'Lothar pushed the ship into hyperdrive and it sped forward faster than the speed of light. . . .' The story is fascinating, so long as one does not balk at the initial impossibility.[11]

Such charges are common to those readers of Kant suddenly confronted with his doctrine of the 'essential ends'. However, in the remainder of this section, I shall try to show that Kant's doctrine, while not all that we might desire, is not as absurd as it is usually taken to be. I shall explain what Kant means by calling happiness and perfection essential ends of humanity, and shall then attempt to show that his critics are correct in claiming that a derivation of these ends from the Categorical Imperative is not possible. I shall argue that this is not because of a failure of the Categorical Imperative, however, because these ends provide the natural framework whereby the very application of the Categorical Imperative is to be achieved. We can hardly expect such riders to a principle to be deduced from that principle itself. And the Categorical Imperative needs to have its doctrine of moral universalisation spelled out in terms of certain ends. Happiness and perfection, like freedom, will perform this function. But we can hardly expect these ends, any more than freedom, to be derived from the notion of universalisation itself.

In the *Metaphysics of Morals*, Kant wants to claim that those ends which are essential to humanity are those ends which men *necessarily* pursue 'considered merely as men' (466 ff.; Gregor, 138 ff.). Man is an animal endowed with reason, and those ends which are essentially human are not those either exclusively animal or exclusively rational. Wealth cannot be an essential end of humanity, because not all men necessarily seek it. Neither could freedom nor sexual pleasure count as essential ends of humanity. The former (though functioning criteriologically like an essential end) is a purely rational end, whereas the latter is a purely animal end. The situation is quite different with happiness and perfection, however, for these ends are necessarily pursued by man as a finite rational being. Happiness, unlike pleasure, is an harmonious integration of ends on the part of the individual. It can be conceived and achieved only with the aid of reason, but would not be desired independently of animal inclination. This gives happiness its peculiarly human characteristics. Perfection consists in the maximum realisation of one's moral and physical potentialities. This, like happiness, can be an end only for a finitely rational being like man. Animals can entertain no such conception, and fully rational beings have already attained by their nature the perfection which is an end for man.[12]

Now given that these two ends, happiness and perfection, are the fixed and essential ends of humanity, what consequences does this have for morality? It is obvious to suggest, of course, that we add these two essential ends to freedom as limiting conditions upon the moral permissibility of actions. This is, in fact, precisely the interpretation I shall offer. However, the problem arises once again of how, within the Kantian system, we are to justify such a move. For, as mentioned previously, Kant makes no effort to derive these ends from the Categorical Imperative. Yet (so someone might argue) some such derivation would seem necessary if it is to be shown that these ends are not merely natural ends but are also ethical ends. For surely it is not the case that we are to respect any end just because it is natural. Some other argument is needed to show which classes of natural ends are also morally relevant. And this argument Kant does not really provide.

Now I do not pretend that any such argument can be given within the Kantian framework. However, it is possible to defend Kant's omission of such an argument roughly in the following way: From the Categorical Imperative we can derive happiness and perfection as ends which we are obligated to promote. However, what cannot be done is to derive from the Categorical Imperative that the pursuit of these ends is more *essential*, given human nature, than the pursuit of other ends, e.g. peace. This can only be established by virtue of what we know of the teleological order in nature. And Kant simply takes it to be a fact that these ends, and no others, are essential to man as a finite rational creature in nature. We cannot really expect Kant to derive the essentiality of these ends from the Categorical Imperative, since these ends themselves provide riders – necessary anthropological (and thus non-moral) supplements – whereby the Categorical Imperative itself can be applied to men as a criterion of right. For exactly the same reason, freedom cannot be derived as an end or value from the Categorical Imperative. The Categorical Imperative commands a harmony of purpose among men. And it seems clear that such a harmony cannot be achieved if those ends which a man necessarily pursues as a finite rational being may be thwarted with impunity. No harmony of purpose could obtain in a world in which men would be subject to arbitrary interference with their happiness and perfection. These two ends (along with freedom) are what make human life worth living. And, once we know this, *then* we know why acting against these ends is immoral. To force a man to sacrifice *necessary* ends, the sacrifice of which he could not himself rationally will, would be to commit a gross immorality. It would be to treat him as a thing, not a person.

In summary, the Categorical Imperative commands that action leave each rational being alone and free to pursue whatever ends he values. The application of the Categorical Imperative will thus be governed in application by those ends which human beings value, but it cannot determine *a priori* what these ends will be in fact. This latter issue is to be decided only by an examination of the nature of man.[13] In Kant's view, the results of such an examination reveal that two ends are essential to human nature – happiness and perfection. Thus, in framing a criterion for moral right, we must take account of the following ends as limiting conditions on the freedom of action of each man: freedom (rational end), happiness and perfection (essential ends of humanity).

We are now in a position to state Kant's account of moral right. Nowhere does Kant state this explicitly, but from the passages examined above, I offer the following criterion as the most plausible interpretation:

> X is a right action if and only if the maxim of X would not, if a universal law, interfere with the freedom of any individual rational being to pursue his own ends in action *so long as these ends do not include the denial of freedom to others to pursue their essential ends – happiness and perfection.*

With this criterion, we are able to handle the case of the homosexual mentioned previously. Private homosexual activities, though perhaps causing disgust to those who know about them, do not interfere with the freedom of other people to seek their own happiness and perfection. This is true for two reasons. First, since the activities are performed in private, they can hardly be called invasions of freedom in any but a Pickwickian sense. Second, even if the bare knowledge that such activities are going on does cause people disgust, the avoidance of such disgust is not an end which is so closely tied with human nature that, if thwarted, it prevents sane men from seeking their happiness or perfection. To regard it so would not entail merely a limitation on freedom; it would entail the elimination of freedom entirely. As H. L. A. Hart has argued in a similar context:

> It may be said that the distress occasioned by the bare thought that others are offending in private against morality cannot constitute 'harm', except in a few neurotic or hypersensitive persons who are literally 'made ill' by this thought. Others may admit such distress is harm, even in the case of normal persons, but argue that it is too slight to outweigh the great misery caused by the legal enforcement of sexual morality.

Although these objections are not without force,

they are of subsidiary importance. The fundamental objection surely is that a right to be protected from the distress which is inseparable from the bare knowledge that others are acting in ways you think wrong, cannot be acknowledged by anyone who recognises individual liberty as a value.... To punish people for causing this form of distress would be tantamount to punishing them simply because others object to what they do.[14]

We have, then, our criterion. However, before considering its implications for political ethics, it will be useful to reflect on it briefly in order to clear up some possible misunderstandings.

First, it is important to see that, as formulated, the criterion reveals a respect for the value of freedom at two points. Most obviously, it teaches that a moral act may not itself be an invasion of freedom. But, and more subtly, it also teaches that a moral action must be such that the freedom to perform it can be extended to all rational beings in similar circumstances. This is the practical output of the notion of moral universalisation. In short, Kant is saying that one who morally respects freedom will be neither an aggressor nor a parasite. So in addition to such obvious invasions of freedom as robbing, raping and murdering, the criterion rules out as immoral such acts as breaking promises for convenience and refusing to obey laws merely because one dislikes them. For these acts, though not aggressive, interfere with freedom in that liberty to perform them is not compatible with a like liberty for all.[15]

Now note that, contrary to much traditional interpretation of Kant, some of the *unintended consequences* of one's actions are clearly of moral relevance in determining the rightness of those actions – at least with regard to perfect duties. Kant is not telling us merely to plan to leave others' freedom secure; he is telling us to leave it secure *in fact*. Whether or not an act of mine would be compatible with a like liberty for others is something capable of an objective determination and is not a function solely of my intentions.

Admittedly, Kant very often does limit his discussion (particularly in the *Foundations*) to intended consequences, those present in my plans or maxims. But this is too narrow. It is, of course, immoral to harm others with such an intention. But it is also immoral to harm others *knowingly, recklessly* or *negligently*. And thus more than what I intend is relevant to the rightness of what I do. Kant, against the utilitarians, rightly wants to consider as morally relevant only those consequences which can be legitimately imputed to the agent (as part of his action), for it would be unjust to hold a man responsible for the remote and accidental consequences of his acts. It would go to an opposite extreme, however, to limit responsibility to intended consequences alone. And so when Kant seems to impose such a limitation in the *Foundations* it is puzzling. But when we move from the worries of the *Foundations*, so tied up with considerations of personal virtue, to the worries about objective rightness which characterise Kant's social philosophy as presented in the *Rechtslehre*, it is significant that this emphasis on intention drops out:

> Justice ... is the aggregate of those conditions under which the will of one person can be conjoined with the will of another in accordance with a universal law of freedom. Every action is just [right] that *in itself* or in its maxim [note: not just 'in its maxim'] is such that the freedom of the will of each can coexist together with the freedom of everyone in accordance with a universal law.... For anyone can still be free even though I am quite indifferent to his freedom or even though I might wish in my heart to infringe on his freedom, as long as I do not through an *external action* violate his freedom.... Hence, the universal law of justice is: act externally in such a way that the free use of your will is compatible with the freedom of everyone according to a universal law (*Justice*, 230–1; Ladd, 34–5 – italics my own).

Thus, with respect at any rate to questions of right or justice, some actual consequences clearly are morally relevant. Kant, of course, wants the Categorical Imperative to test the morality of actions *before* they are performed so that we can use the criterion to make moral decisions. And it might seem that for this reason we can consider only intended consequences, those present in actual plans. But this would be a mistake if for no other reason than that it would encourage immoral negligence by discouraging the use of rational foresight in formulating plans or maxims. Thus perhaps we might follow the lead of positive law and objectify the maxim, i.e. regard the maxim of an action as the plan, not merely as the agent sees it, but as a reasonable man would see it (and thus how the agent *ought* to see it). This ties rightness to culpability without going to the extreme of tying it to intention alone.

It is also important to note that, though consequences are relevant for Kant, they are not relevant in the way the utilitarian thinks they are. For the utilitarian, an action is wrong if and because the consequences are bad (act utilitarianism) or if and because it violates a rule with good consequences (rule utilitarianism). But Kant will have none of this, for his interest is in justice or fairness. It is by being treated unjustly that men are wronged, are treated as means. And so Kant's interest in consequences extends only in so far as they serve to bring out a certain kind of injustice. For if the consequences of everyone's doing X would be morally undesirable, it is immoral for me to do it. This is not because the consequences are bad in fact (they might not be) or because the act violates a good rule (there may be no rule) but because, given the bad consequences that would follow if everyone did X, in doing X I am taking a liberty that I could not rationally extend to all others.[16] And so Kant, unlike the utilitarian, is not concerned with the *probability* of certain consequences. The utilitarian argument is, at most, an argument to show that if you want to act in a certain way that not everyone could act in (break a promise, say), you should keep your action well hidden so that others will not be tempted to follow your example. And so the utilitarian, unlike Kant, cannot explain why it is immoral to break a promise even when you *know* that others will keep theirs.

Thus Kant, though strikingly anti-utilitarian, is not nearly so anti-teleological, so opposed to all consequential considerations, as generally interpreted. He depreciates happiness in favour of freedom, utility in favour of justice; but he does not rule out consequences entirely. But the utilitarian, concerned with consequences *simpliciter*, asks the question 'What will it be like if...?' Kant, concerned with justice, asks the question 'What *would* it be like if...?' And the importance of considering consequences in this way is to bring out the possibility that some action you perform may be unjust because you could not rationally allow others to do it. The question 'Could I extend this liberty to all men?' can be answered, at least sometimes, only by a consideration of the consequences of such an extension.[17] What other difference is there between the permissible liberty of doing isometric exercises in my office and the impermissible liberty of cheating on my income tax return except that the consequences of everyone doing the former would be indifferent and the consequences of everyone doing the latter would be bad? And so the liberty of doing private exercises is a liberty I can extend to all men, whereas the liberty to lie in declaring income is not.

Before proceeding, it might be useful to present a brief summary of the foregoing in a reasonably non-Kantian idiom. In outline, I have been arguing for the following: Kant's fundamental characterisation of a morally right action is that it is an action which, if made a general policy, would leave secured the freedom of other rational beings. This provides the essence of a morally right action. However, in attempting to use the essence of morality alone as a criterion for man, we run into certain problems. For example, we seem to have no justification for preventing the abuse of freedom – a vice quite common to humanity. Kant's solution to this problem lies in his doctrine of the moral title, i.e. there is a moral title or authority to interfere with the abuse of freedom, for, in so doing, we place an 'obstacle to an obstacle' to freedom. This is one way to value freedom and is, as a practice, derivable from the Categorical Imperative – though Kant does not himself perform the derivation. However, the moral title raises problems of its own. For how are we to know when an abuse of freedom is severe enough to justify intervention? We want to defend freedom without being moral busybodies. At this point, we can make use of Kant's doctrine of the essential ends of humanity. These ends (happiness and perfection) allow us to define a real violation of freedom. Only when they are acted against by an agent is it morally justified to limit that agent's freedom. The essentiality of these ends is not, of course, derivable from the Categorical Imperative. Rather happiness and perfection are, like freedom, non-moral values which function as limiting conditions on the morality of actions. They are unlike freedom, however, in that they are not essentially (definitionally) but are only criteriologically tied to morality. They enable us to spell out what counts as valuing freedom *in humanity*, but they would be irrelevant with respect to other rational beings of different constitution.

Now there is one question about the moral title that has so far been ignored: *who* has the title to prevent abuses of freedom? Kant's view, one of the central views of his entire political theory, is that only a social institution may have this authority, *not* an individual. So just because Jones is acting wrongly, it does not follow that *I* have the title or authority to interfere with him. He ought to be interfered with surely, but only by an appropriate agency founded on fairness in procedure. The nature and implications of this position will be explored in the final chapter.

4 Justice and the Rule of Law

Introduction

Kant's *Metaphysical Elements of Justice* (*Rechtslehre*) is largely devoted to what is surely the basic problem of political ethics: the nature and justification of *coercion*. And this is a problem which Kant, given his presentation of freedom as the basic value of morality, must come to grips with in a careful way. For Kant's defence of freedom has in effect been an attempt to establish a formal principle for locating the burden of proof in discussions of coercion. Kant quite clearly believes that freedom does not stand in need of any positive justification, for it is good in itself. Rather it is coercion, bad in itself, which must be defended.[1] The burden of proof lies on the man who would interfere with the freedom of another. But this is not yet to say very much of political substance; for, after locating the burden of proof, we still need to know when that burden has been successfully borne by the man who would advocate coercion.

In our discussion thus far, we have a hint as to Kant's substantive view. This view, expressed in the doctrine of the moral title, is that coercion is justified only in so far as it is used to prevent invasions against freedom. Freedom itself is the only value which can be used to limit freedom, for the use of any other value (e.g. utility) would undermine the ultimate status of the value of freedom. So Kant has to establish the paradoxical claim that some forms of coercion (as opposed to violence) are morally permissible because, contrary to appearance, they really *expand* rational freedom. And he will argue roughly in the following way: Coercion may keep people from doing what they

109

desire to do on a particular occasion and is thus *prima facie* wrong. However, such coercion can be shown to be morally justified, and thus *only prima facie* wrong, if it can be established that the coercion is such that it could have been rationally willed even by the person whose desire is interfered with:

> Accordingly, when it is said that a creditor has a right to demand from his debtor the payment of a debt, this does not mean that he can *persuade* the debtor that his own reason itself obligates him to this performance; on the contrary, to say that he has such a right means only that the use of coercion to make anyone do this is entirely compatible with everyone's freedom, *including the freedom of the debtor*, in accordance with universal laws.

> To say 'I will to be punished if I murder someone' can mean nothing more than 'I submit myself along with everyone else to those laws which, if there are any criminals among the people, will naturally include penal laws' (*Justice*, 232, 335; Lad, 37, 105 – italics my own).

Like Rousseau, Kant thinks that it is only in a context governed by social practice (particularly civil government with its Rule of Law) that this can make sense. Laws may require of Jones some action that he does not desire to perform. This is not a violent invasion of his freedom, however, if it can be shown that, in some antecedent position of choice, he would have been rational to adopt a Rule of Law (and thus run the risk of having some desire thwarted) rather than some other alternative arrangement like the classical state of nature. This is, indeed, the only sense that Kant is able to make of classical social contract theory. Such theories are to be viewed, not as historical fantasies, but as ideal models of rational decision. For what these theories actually claim is that the only coercive institutions that are morally justified are those which a group of rational beings could agree to adopt in a position of having to pick social institutions to govern their relations:

> The contract, which is called *contractus originarius*, or *pactum sociale* ... need not be assumed to be a fact, indeed it is not [even possible as such. To suppose that would be like insisting] that before anyone would be bound to respect such a civic constitution, it be proved first of all from history that a people, whose rights and obligations we have entered into as their descendants, had *once upon a time* executed such an act and had left a reliable document or instrument, either orally or in writing, concerning this contract. Instead, this contract is a *mere idea* of reason which has undoubted practical reality; namely, to oblige every legislator to give us laws in such a manner that the laws *could* have originated from the united will of the entire people and to regard every subject in so far as he is a citizen as though he had consented to such [an expression of the general] will. This is the testing stone of the rightness of every publicly-known law, for if a law were such that it was impossible for an entire people to give consent to it (as for example a law that a certain class of subjects, by inheritance, should have the privilege of the *status of lords*), then such a law is unjust. On the other hand, if there is a mere *possibility* that a people might consent to a (certain) law, then it is a duty to consider that the law is just, even though at the moment the people might be in such a position or have a point of view that would result in their refusing to give their consent to it if asked (*Theory and Practice*, 297; Friedrich, 421–2).

The problem of organising a state, however hard it may seem, can be solved even for a race of devils, if only they are intelligent. The problem is: 'Given a multiple of rational beings requiring universal laws for their preservation, but each of whom is secretly inclined to exempt himself from them, to establish a constitution in such a way that, although their private intentions conflict, they check each other, with the result that their public conduct is the same as if they had no such intentions' (*Perpetual Peace*, 366; Beck, 112).[2]

Thus Kant's doctrine of the moral title, though similar to Mill's later self-protection principle,[3] is really quite different in substance. For though Kant in some general sense argues that coercion is justified only to prevent harm to others, he understands by 'harm' only certain invasions of freedom and not simply disutility.[4] Also, his defence of the principle is not grounded, as is Mill's, in *its* social utility. Rather it is to be regarded as a principle of justice, by which Kant means a principle that rational beings could adopt in a situation of mutual choice:

The concept [of justice] applies only to the relationship of a will to another person's will, not to his wishes or desires (or even just his needs) which are the concern of acts of benevolence and charity.... In applying the concept of justice we take into consideration only the form of the relationship between the wills insofar as they are regarded as free, and whether the action of one of them can be conjoined with the freedom of the other in accordance with universal law. Justice is therefore the aggregate of those conditions under which the will of one person can be conjoined with the will of another in accordance with a universal law of freedom (*Justice*, 230; Ladd, 34).

Though Kant, unlike such later writers in jurisprudence as Austin or Kelsen, has no elaborated descriptive theory of the nature of law as a social institution, he does seem to embrace a generally positivistic account. That is, he regards law as a normative order which functions as a coercive system of social control. And as such, it clearly stands in need of justification. It is Kant's firm view that the only good justification will lie in principles of justice rather than utility.

Now to argue that coercion is to be justified only to prevent an interference with freedom is still to leave open one central question: *Who* is justified in applying the coercion? Though it may be true that Jones, who has invaded Smith's freedom, ought to be punished, it does not follow that *I* or any other individual has the moral right to impose the punishment. And indeed Kant is emphatic in his insistence that individuals do *not* have such a moral right; for the right is properly ascribed only to some duly constituted legal authority. This places Kant in sharp contrast to a writer like Locke, who made the *natural* right of each man to punish the cornerstone of his entire political theory. And thus, as a way of bringing Kant's theory into sharper focus, it will be illuminating to discuss Locke's justification for civil government (a largely *utilitarian* justification, significantly enough) and the Kantian reply to that justification.[5] Having understood Kant's own moral justification for government and its Rule of Law, we can then consider Kant's views on the form that government ought to take and on the rights and obligations that government and its citizens have vis-à-vis one another.

Locke's Theory and the Kantian Reply

Central to Locke's justification for the passage from a pre-civil to a civil society is his claim that we have a natural right to punish, a natural right (as he sometimes calls it) of 'execution'. This is the principal right that we provisionally give up or entrust to the civil society – all the rights of legitimate government being *acquired* and taking the form of a trust from the participating citizens. The relationship between citizens and their legitimate government is fiduciary, not contractual. We have in a state of nature the right to punish, to execute the law of nature, but this right is exercised inefficiently, in a disutilitarian fashion. It presents, to use Locke's own phrase, a great 'inconvenience' (13).[6] Thus, in order to secure a more utilitarian practice of punishment, we entrust this power to civil society, to the machinery of government.

Such is the general structure of Locke's argument.

113

Unfortunately, however, it involves a debilitating paradox. For the notion of a natural right to punish, in a sense of 'punish' strong enough to count as an entrusted governmental right, is unintelligible. It is not simply that such punishing in a state of nature is inefficient; it is conceptually impossible. For punishment, as Hobbes noted, is paradigmatically a legalistic institution. Thus, upon any plausible interpretation of punishment, it is wrong to say that we have a natural right to punish. And thus it is impossible to appeal to this right in a trust justification for legitimate civil society. The only situation in which it might appear to make sense to say that punishment could exist in a pre-civil society would be a situation in which all the participating beings were fully rational, all knowing and all good. But this, though perhaps the only situation in which a claim for such a natural right is tempting, describes just that kind of community which would not *need* civil government. So, put shortly, the paradox is simply this: It is unintelligible to claim that normal human beings (who stand in need of civil government) have a natural right to punish. Only perfectly good and wise beings (who do not stand in such need) could perhaps be said to have such a right. Locke cannot have it both ways. Thus no claim about a natural right to punish can intelligibly be used in a justification for the transition from a pre-civil to a civil society.

Now in order to see the important place in Locke's political theory of the notion of a natural right to punish, one may begin by considering some of the passages where he describes the fiduciary nature of legitimate government:

The liberty of man in society is to be under no other legislative power but that established by consent of the commonwealth, nor under the dominion of any will, or restraint of any law, but what the legislative shall enact according to the trust put in it (22). For it [the legislative], being but the joint power of every member of the society given up to that person or assembly which is legislator, can be no more than

114

those persons had in a state of nature before they entered into society, and gave it up to the community. For nobody can transfer to another more power than he has in himself (135).

Locke's whole justification for revolution (conceived as the return to the people of what is rightfully theirs) is closely tied to his view that government, if legitimate, has only that authority which is entrusted to it by the citizens it serves. And citizens can entrust to government only that which they themselves possess. Thus, in order to see if Locke's view is coherent, it is necessary to make the following two investigations: First, it must be determined just what powers or rights are constitutive of civil government – that is, just what powers must necessarily be present in any social body if that body may properly be called a civil government. (The contrast here is with powers which a particular government might, as a matter of fact, have but which would not be necessary for the correct application of the concept of civil government, e.g. the power to tax for highway construction.) Second, an investigation is required into the extent to which it is intelligible to say that these rights or powers could be held by citizens in a state of nature – that is, outside of the conventional institutional context of civil government. For any power which cannot intelligibly be assigned to citizens in a state of nature presumably cannot be entrusted by those citizens to a ruling government. You cannot give up what you have not got.

Now Locke is quite clear in presenting those conditions he takes to be constitutive of civil government. These conditions, which would be fully endorsed by Kant, are generally definitive of what may be called the Rule of Law:

Those who are united into one body, and have a common established law and judicature to appeal to, with authority to decide controversies between them and punish offenders, are in civil society one with another. All private judgment of every particular member being excluded, the community comes to be umpire, by settled standing rules; indifferent and the same to all parties (87). In the state of nature there are many things wanting. First, there wants an established, settled, known law received and allowed by common consent to be the standard of right and wrong, and the common measure to decide all controversies (124). Second, there wants an indifferent and known judge, with authority to determine all differences according to the established law (125). Thirdly, there wants power to back and support the sentence when right, and to give it due execution (126).

Note that these conditions are procedural conditions for the enactment, application and enforcement of rules for the ordering of social behaviour. Thus the Rule of Law provides each citizen with rules which serve as standards for the regulation of his affairs. Complete with a system of sanctions, they give him reasonable expectations about his future in that they allow him to avoid proscribed behaviour and (though Locke says far too little about this) to acquire and exercise powers. And this is indeed a plausible minimum characterisation of what would constitute a system of positive law. As Locke himself notes (12), a system of legal rules can be viewed, at least minimally, as a price system on human conduct.

The enacted rules stipulate the price (a certain degree of punishment). But just as a price system can function only in so far as the price specified is indeed generally charged, so too can a system of legal rules function only if the rules and the penalties they involve are consistently enforced through procedures of authoritative application. This is why, as John Rawls has stressed,[7] a system of punishment must make a practice of inflicting sanctions only upon those who are *guilty* of violations. For my ability to use the law to regulate my own conduct necessarily involves the reasonable belief on my part that my suffering punishment will depend in large measure upon whether or not I have really committed a delict and not, for example, upon someone's belief that I have done something wrong or that I present a danger to the community. And so it is a necessary truth about the institutional rules prescribing punishment, and not merely a moral observation about them, that they should be justly enforced – that like cases be treated alike. For only in this way can law attain its prime social function: the control of social behaviour through rules. And thus if the traditional natural-law claim that 'an unjust law is not law' is changed to 'an unjustly enforced law is not law', then an important insight about the nature of law itself is indeed being made.

To put the point briefly: Legal systems are systems of rules for the regulation of social behaviour. These rules can perform their function only if coupled with a justly enforced system of authoritative punishment. *Punishment* is necessary both to provide an incentive for obedience and to guarantee that those who voluntarily obey will not unfairly suffer as a result of disobedience by others. Punishment must be *authoritative*, because only in this way can punishment proper be distinguished from the kind of infliction of social harm that is found, for example, in the activities of certain vigilante groups. As Hobbes remarks, 'neither private revenges, nor injuries of private men, can properly be styled punishment; because they proceed not from public authority' (*Leviathan*, chapter xxviii). Finally, punishment must be *justly enforced* if the rules which punishment sanctions are indeed to regulate conduct. For a rule which is arbitrarily enforced, or which allows sanctions to fall upon the citizens in the absence of a breach of the rule, could hardly be appealed to as a *standard* at all. The citizen in such a society would be advised to ignore the rules entirely and concentrate instead on attempting to form generalisations about how officials *do* behave, forgetting about how – according to the rules – they *ought* to behave.

The need for the Rule of Law, then, figures in the justification for any civil society at all. The requirement that civil society may properly claim only those rights or powers which the citizen can entrust to it in part explicates Locke's notion of *legitimate* civil society. Both claims are crucial to Locke's total theory.

The problem which faces Locke's theory, then, is now quite clear: What sense, if any, can be made of the claim that human beings have, in a state of nature, a right to punish? Punishment demands, at a minimum, three conditions: a system of rules, authorities to apply these rules, and authorities to enforce sanctions for breaches of these rules. These latter two conditions distinguish the mere infliction of social harm (e.g. vigilante activity) from punishment proper. So our question, to what extent is it intelligible to say that people have a natural right to punish, will depend upon the degree to which in a state of nature we have reasonable analogues to these three conditions. And my argument will be that, at most, Locke can present a reasonable analogue to the first condition: the existence of a system of rules. By attempting to establish analogues to the second and third conditions, however, he manages to break down the very distinction which is crucial to an understanding of punishment – namely, the distinction between punishing a man and merely (even if conscientiously) harming him.

Now Locke feels that, just as in civil society we are bound by the positive law, so in the state of nature each man is bound by the natural law – teleological rules of conduct for the direction of his activities laid down by God and discoverable by human reason (6). To say that the existence and discoverability of such rules is controversial would be an extreme act of philosophical charity. But a general external objection to natural law as such is beside my present purpose. Suffice it merely to point out that in speaking of such rules Locke is revealing a sensitivity to one of the requirements he must meet if his claim for a natural right to punish is to be intelligible. For punishment is, minimally, the infliction of harm for the breach of rules. This is why phrases like 'The Land-Rover can take a lot of punishment' represent secondary uses of punishment language – that is, uses which can, without loss of sense, be replaced by talk about mere harm.

And surely all that we mean by the claim in question is that the vehicle can survive a great deal of abuse – not that it, in any way, comes into conflict with any social rules.

When we come to the other conditions, however, the poverty of Locke's claim is strikingly revealed. For what sense can we give to the notion, in a state of nature, of *authoritative* interpretation of law and infliction of harm? Just, according to Locke, the following:

> The execution of the law of nature is (in the state of nature) put into every man's hands, whereby every one has a right to punish the transgressors of that law to such a degree as may hinder its violation (7). Man hath by nature a power not only to preserve his property, that is, his life, liberty and estate, against the injuries and attempts of other men, but to judge of and punish the breaches of that law in others, as he is persuaded the offence deserves, even with death itself, in crimes where the heinousness of the act, in his opinion, requires it (87).

Here is Locke's description of the natural right to punish. And it is, unfortunately for his theory, absolutely indistinguishable from vigilante activity. Surely the white racist, organising with his compatriots for the lynching of some black man who has committed the 'crime' of befriending a white woman, is himself *persuaded* that the act deserves harm. He does not, at least not normally, act contrary to his own *opinion* in the matter. So surely mere conscientiousness does not give a man the authority to punish. And this is so, in part, for purely logical reasons: If we say that each man in a state of nature is an authority with respect to punishment, then when Jones says 'Martin deserves punishment' and Smith says 'Martin does not deserve punishment', they are *both* – if equally conscientious – issuing binding judgments. But this is incoherent. Where everyone is said to be an authority, the concept of authority operates without sense.

There is one sort of objection that needs to be considered here. It might be suggested that people in a state of nature presumably can have a language and that, if they can, then this shows that they can be counted on to distinguish correct applications of rules from incorrect applications. So why can they not be counted on to do this with respect to punishment? I have several answers to this: First, the issue with punishment is not merely correctness of judgment but the supposed right to *act* (and thereby cause harm to others) on the basis of the judgment. And so the issue has a moral import lacking in a question of the mere linguistic correctness of judgment. Second, the judgments in question here are going to be *evaluative* in character. And, as C. L. Stevenson and others have reminded us, radical disagreement is possible with respect to judgments of this sort. So even if people in a state of nature can have sufficient agreement on paradigm cases to allow them to understand and use the expression 'deserves punishment', it does not follow from this that they can in general be said to have a moral right to act on their judgments in this regard. Finally, the authority which a native speaker can be said to have over at least a part of his language is *expert* authority, whereas the authority to punish is *performative* authority. That is, a native speaker can be counted on to make *correct* judgments (as Hoyle can be counted on to make correct claims about the rules of games), whereas authorities to punish issue *binding* judgments (as the Pope issues binding judgments on Catholic dogma). That these concepts are different is easily illustrated by the fact that a binding judgment ('Jones is guilty' declared by a judge) may fail to be correct (Jones, in point of fact, did not commit the act).

To summarise, then, what Locke describes as a natural right to punish is not descriptive of punishment at all, for it describes a practice in which everyone, at all times, has authority to inflict harm for felt wrongs. This is not punishment but merely the exercise of vigilante force – something we are surely able to do but nothing we have a right to do. And even if we did have this right, it cannot be the right the *entrusting* of

120

which creates civil punishment. For civil punishment is not, in any important way, even analogous to vigilante force. (And it is considerably *more* than family punishment. Thus the fact that fathers may be said to punish their children even in a state of nature does not affect our argument in the least – as is revealed by the fact that fathers may *still* do this even in civil society.)

Now this objection to Locke is not merely verbal. That is, it will not do to reply by claiming that, though it is misleading to say that there is a natural right to punish, there is a natural right to do that which, if it did occur in civil society, would be called punishment. This will not wash. For the distinction that is relevant here is not merely a verbal distinction, but a distinction in kind which can be marked by categories of moral justification. Of two practices P_1 and P_2, it would be odd to say that they differed merely in verbal description if it were true that P_1 is morally justified and P_2 is not. And yet this is precisely the situation we face in contrasting so-called natural punishment with civil or legal punishment. For few of us have any doubts that a system of legal punishment is morally justified – primarily in terms of the personal protection it obtains for all. (Though we can, of course, disagree over just what activities should be punished and what the sanctions should be.) But I do not think that any reasonable man could regard as justified a system in which harm could be inflicted at will by any person so long as that person merely *thought* that another was deserving. For since no man desires to suffer unjustly at the hands of another, it would be irrational for any man to acknowledge as a justifiable social policy a practice which would render such suffering likely.

I conclude, then, that it is unintelligible to say that people have a natural right to punish. It might make some sense to say that there is a limited natural right to self-defence; but since civil punishment is more than self-defence, the surrender of the right of self-defence will not be sufficient to *entrust* the right of punishment to civil society. In accepting punishment as a legal institution, we do give up our right to self-defence – at least in those areas where we have an appeal to legal redress. But to say that in accepting some institution P we give up right R is considerably weaker than saying that P is just R entrusted.

At this point it might be well to consider a possible Lockean reply to this line of argument. Locke would, I think, want to argue that the initial objection we all feel to the claim that there is a natural right to punish is merely utilitarian and not conceptual. What really worries us is that the exercise of natural punishment will have morally bad consequences. It is not wrong *simpliciter* for a man to be judge and executioner with respect to his own case; it is only immoral if this man acts in an uninformed and biased fashion. But if we remember that men in a state of nature know the law of nature through reason and recognise that they are bound by it, this difficulty does not really arise.

Now the line of reply here suggested is quite self-defeating. Locke often does speak of the pre-civil society being reasonably peaceful because its citizens recognise the law of nature in governing their affairs. He does not believe that the state of nature is necessarily a state of war wherein life is nasty, brutish and short. (This is in contrast, not only to Hobbes but also to other passages in the *Second Treatise* where Locke is trying to demonstrate just how badly men need civil government.) So perhaps, if this is kept in mind, what has been described as a natural right to punish will not describe an immoral practice after all, since most citizens are under the guidance of reason and will thus not typically act in a disutilitarian fashion. Though this right (since it rests on expert rather than performative authority) is somewhat misleadingly called 'punishment', this objection may now appear merely verbal because the practice in question is, even if inconvenient, not grossly immoral:

> It is certain that there is a law of nature, and that it is as intelligible and plain to a rational creature, and a studier of that law, as the positive laws of commonwealths: nay, possibly plainer; as much as

reason is easier to be understood, than the fancies and intricate contrivances of men, following contrary and hidden interests put into words (12).

Unfortunately, this line of reply, if it proves anything at all, proves too much to serve Locke's purpose. It proves nothing unless we grant Locke the dubious assumption that people who know the right will generally *act* on the basis of this knowledge. But if we grant him this, the following troublesome consequence arises: These fine fellows now imagined as having a natural right to punish have, because of that wisdom and virtue which allows them the right, precious little *need* for civil society. They are, indeed, rather like Kant's conception of fully rational beings. Since a few of these beings may occasionally lapse, it might be somewhat more convenient for them to have civil government, but mere convenience will hardly bear the moral load that has traditionally been placed on natural rights. As Margaret Macdonald has observed in a similar context, 'it could, perhaps, be proved hedonistically that life for most ordinary citizens is more *comfortable* in a democratic society. But would an appeal for effort, on this ground, have been sanctioned between 1939 and 1945? However true, it would have been rejected as insufficient because *uninspired*. Who could be moved to endure 'blood, toil, tears and sweat' for the sake of a little extra comfort?'[8]

Now what is ironic here is that Locke's particular confusion over the natural right to punish caused him to miss what is perhaps the *best* justification for civil government – a justification captured, however inadequately, in Kant's paradoxical claim that man's freedom is promoted, and not hindered, by law.[9] For Kant saw what Locke failed to see – that in a state of nature one is faced both with a crying need and with the absence of any fair or just way of relieving that need. The need is for security against both personal assaults and the profits of others by one's sacrifice. This need arises from the fact that human beings are not fully rational beings; they are, rather, creatures of limited knowledge and self-restraint. And these same limitations which create the need to punish would surely infect those who would set out to judge and punish on their own. Thus, Kant argues, requirements of justice cannot be satisfied in a state of nature. For though I might be tempted to harm others when I feel that they have done something wrong, I could not adopt this as a universalisable maxim of action since I could not (as justice would demand) consistently assent to the right of others to harm me when they merely thought that I had done something wrong. I could not regard such an invasion of my freedom as justified, and thus I could not rationally commit similar invasions of the freedom of others.

What is needed, then, is a social adjudication procedure upon which all reasonable men could agree. And such a procedure is just civil government. Forming such government is *obligatory* (and not merely permissible) because only in this way can the demands of social justice be secured — the demands that each man's freedom be limited only by considerations that each man could acknowledge as fair. Limitations on freedom in a state of nature are arbitrary and violent. The legitimate limitations on freedom in a properly functioning civil society expand freedom, however, because they *are* limitations which all men could acknowledge as fair. Thus a right is secured in civil society that could not be secured in a state of nature, and this point is merely obscured by the talk of governmental rights as a trust from citizens:

Accordingly, we cannot say that a man has sacrificed in the state a part of his inborn external freedom for some particular purpose; rather, we must say that he has completely abandoned his wild, lawless freedom in order to find his whole freedom again undiminished in a lawful dependency, that is, in a juridical state of society, since this dependency comes from his own legislative Will.... Even if we imagine men to be ever so good-natured and righteous before a public lawful state of society is established, individual men, nations and states can never be certain that they are secure against violence from one another, because each will claim his own right to do what *seems just and good to him,* entirely independently of the opinion of others.... [This] nonjuridical state of affairs, that is one in which there is no distributive legal justice, is called a state of nature.... If you are [situated in such a state] you ought to abandon the state of nature and enter, with all others, a juridical state of affairs, that is, a state of distributive legal justice. The ground of this postulate can be developed analytically from the concept of justice in external relations as contrasted to violence.... No one is bound to refrain from encroaching upon the possession of another man if the latter does not in equal measure guarantee that the same kind of restraint will be exercised with regard to him (*Justice,* 316, 312, 306–7; Ladd, 80–1, 76, 70–1).[10]

Locke's claim is that we have a natural right to punish and that we move to civil government in order to punish more efficiently. Kant's claim, on the other hand, is that we have a natural *need* to punish but no natural right. For presumably I cannot have a natural right to do *A* if the doing of *A* is morally wrong – as the pre-legal infliction of harm for felt wrongs is morally wrong. Our right to outer freedom might be described as the right to acquire rights in general. The right to punish (in the broad sense of executing law) is one of the constitutive properties of government, and our need for government is in part a need for an institution which makes such a right possible. I do not entrust my right to punish to government (since I never had any such right), and thus the justification for government is not to be found in any talk of trust. Rather government, with its Rule of Law, is justified (at least in part) in that it expands my freedom. For in governmental society I am morally free to do something not permissible in a state of nature – namely, seek legitimate redress for wrongs done according to principles which I, and all other rational agents, can acknowledge as fair and therefore as binding.[11]

Kant, then, is opposed to all talk of governmental rights being a kind of trust from the participating citizens. For our only natural or innate right is freedom. Freedom in the natural state is simply the legitimate (but *unguaranteed*) claim that each man has a right to be let alone to do whatever he wants – subject, of course, to the limitation that the same right is extended to others. Politically, however, freedom must be understood as the right to *acquire* rights in general. The entire political sphere consists of acquired rights, and all talk of trust obscures this basic feature of government.[12] For we move to government in order to acquire rights which either (like punishment) do not exist in a state of nature at all or (like property) exist only provisionally. Of course, there are many things it would be *good* to do, because desirable on grounds of utility, in a state of nature. But it does not follow from this alone that we would, in a state of nature, have any moral *right* to do these things. For legitimate talk of such rights can take place only in a context governed by considerations of justice or fairness, and such considerations can be operative only in a context of institutional procedures guaranteeing due process:

> The concept of an external right is derived from the concept of freedom in the external relation of human beings to each other. This concept has nothing at all to do with the purpose which all human beings naturally have; namely, a desire for happiness, nor has it anything to do with the means of achieving such happiness. Thus the desire for happiness must not be included as a ground for determining laws of external right. *Right* is the limitation of every man's freedom so that it harmonises with the freedom of every other man in so far as harmonisation is possible according to a general law (*Theory and Practice*, 289; Friedrich, 415).

> The well-being of the state must not be confused with the welfare or happiness of the citizens of the state, for these can be attained more easily and satisfactorily in a state of nature (as Rousseau maintained) or even under despotic government. By 'the well-being of the state' is meant that condition in

126

which the constitution conforms most closely to the principles of justice (*Justice*, 318; Ladd, 83).

Kant's theory of the nature and justification for government and its Rule of Law, then, stands in sharp contrast to that of both Hobbes and Locke. Hobbes argued that government was to be preferred to the state of nature for reasons of enlightened egoism. Locke argued for its preferability on grounds of utility. Kant finds both of these theories suspect on both scientific and moral grounds. Scientifically, the theories are really fantasies of *a priori* sociology. Who really knows, and how could we ever test through experiment, that people are happier in civil society than in a state of nature? Morally, Kant makes the extremely important point that no amount of happiness or self-interest could establish the moral worth of law and government unless it could also be shown that these institutions are compatible with the demands of freedom and justice. (It is not on grounds of utility, surely, that we condemn the society of *Brave New World*.) Having thus seen the outline of Kant's view, we may now pass to a consideration of some of the details of his theory of law and government.

The Nature of Legitimate Law and Government

As Kant views the state of nature, it is characterised by certain pathologies. In the first place, there is no fair way to guarantee that one natural right we have – freedom. In the second place, there is no way to legitimately acquire other rights and powers. And so government, with its Rule of Law, is to be viewed as a cure for these social pathologies. Government allows the acquisition of a right to punish and thus secures freedom fairly. And it provides a fair way for the exercise of powers that are lacking in a natural state. Kant argues, for example, that there are certain intuitively plausible claims for property (e.g. *de facto* possession) in a state of nature but that these give only provisional rights until guaranteed by law. Thus, even with respect to property, the basic worry is compulsion or coercion. For property is not really mine unless others may be compelled from encroaching on it. But any prelegal compulsion, like punishment, could rest on no fair principle:

> I am not bound to leave what is another's [property] untouched if everyone else does not in turn guarantee to me with regard to what is mine that he will act in accordance with exactly the same principle. . . . With respect to an external and contingent possession, a unilateral Will cannot serve as a coercive law for everyone, since that would be a violation of freedom in accordance with universal laws. Therefore, only a Will binding everyone else – that is, a collective, or universal (common), and powerful Will – is the kind of Will that can provide the guarantee required. The condition of being subject to general external (that is, public) legislation that is backed by power is civil society. Accordingly, a thing can be externally yours or mine only in a civil society (*Justice*, 256; Ladd, 64–5).

Kant's basic position, then, is that the Rule of Law is justified as a cure for *violence* – by which he means not just bodily harm, but any illegitimate interference with freedom. Through providing a binding social decision procedure for resolving conflict, the Rule of Law eliminates the resort to violence as a solution to social controversy. Even when such a procedure does not yield us what we desire, we have no moral complaint against it so long as our claim has been heard and decided fairly. One has not been dealt with unfairly just because one does not get what one wants. Violence is always wrong, but there is a certain *excuse* for resorting to it in a state of nature.[13] When living under a fair procedure for resolving conflict, however, such an excuse is not present. For to adopt a social decision procedure is just to give up the privilege of deciding each case on its own perceived merits.

Now this notion of *excuse* gives us a way of understanding how Kant might deal with some apparent counter-examples to his theory. It might be argued that men have a right to act violently on certain occasions. For example, most of us do not condemn acts of self-defence – violence which meets attack from another person. Similarly, a so-called 'right of necessity' has often been invoked to defend people who, for example, throw one man overboard on a lifeboat so that the rest can be saved. Now Kant's view is that this conduct is morally wrong but, under the circumstances, can be regarded as excusable. It is wrong, because it cannot be willed a universal law. I could not will to be in the place of the man sacrificed, and so it is unjust and therefore immoral to advocate such treatment for others. However, under extreme circumstances, we can understand the pressures operative and excuse, at least partially, the performance of such wrong acts and so judge less harshly the *people* involved. So the location 'right of necessity' is misleading because it describes, not a real moral right, but an excusable moral wrong. And it is a recognition of the pressures operative on a man in these situations which would make it unreasonable to punish a man for this kind of wrongdoing:

It is clear that this allegation [of a right based on necessity] is not to be understood objectively, according to what a law might prescribe, but merely subjectively, as the sentence might be pronounced in a court of law. There could be no penal law assigning the death penalty to a man who has been shipwrecked and finds himself struggling with another man – both in equal danger of losing their lives – and who, in order to save his own life, pushes the other man off the plank on which he had saved himself. For the first man, no punishment threatened by the law could be greater than losing his life. A penal law applying to such a situation could never have the effect intended, for the threat of an evil that is still uncertain (being condemned to death by a judge) cannot outweigh the fear of an evil that is certain (being drowned). Hence, we must judge that, although an act of self-preservation

129

through violence is not inculpable, it is still unpunishable (*Justice*, 235: Ladd, 41).

Why is it wrong to punish in these situations? For two reasons, really, one practical and the other moral. The practical reason is revealed in the realisation that the law is a kind of price system. Since no price the law could charge can possibly outweigh the consequence of avoiding the violent act, it appears unreasonable to enact the price since it could not have had that kind of control over the agent's behaviour that a price system is supposed to have. The moral reason is one of fairness. Since none of us could be sure of exercising any greater restraint under similar circumstances, it is unfair to demand such restraint from others.[14]

So though violence may under extreme circumstances be excusable, it is never justifiable and is thus always morally wrong. The coercion of other people is only justified if carried out through the procedural channels of a fair Rule of Law, and in the absence of such procedures your duty is restraint. If there are such proceedings, and you lose in using them, you have no moral complaint to lodge – and certainly no complaint that would justify a resort to violence.

Thus Kant's theory enshrines the basic strengths and the basic weaknesses of classical liberalism. He has an intense faith in procedural forms and a belief that all injustice can be dealt with in terms of a fair system of law. There is an important insight here but there is also, of course, an important oversight. For fairness in procedure is merely a formal guarantee and, as such, necessarily ignores certain substantive considerations. Like rules of a game, fairness as a legal principle operates with respect to formally defined place-holders in a social system. But what does one do when some of those place-holders, because of social rather than legal reasons, operate under a built-in disadvantage? This, after all, was Marx's later criticism of industrial capitalism. Workers had no formal complaint against the system of laws under which they lived. But they still had a moral complaint because certain social and economic factors put them at a disadvantage in the effective use of those procedures. Is this not a moral defect of an important nature, one properly called an injustice?[15]

Now Kant has a very superficial answer to this worry. He argues that this objection can still be handled with a formal procedure – roughly a procedure which allows that those presently disadvantaged may not be permanently disadvantaged. To guarantee this, we have to make the positions and offices in society in principle open to all so that any man can 'work up' to a status of full participation:

> A civil constitution only provides the juridical condition under which each person's property is secured and guaranteed to him, but it does not actually stipulate and determine what that property shall be.... [Also] from the fact that [passive citizens] can still demand that they be treated by others in accordance with the laws of natural freedom and equality it does not follow that they have a right as active members to guide the state, to organise, and to work for the introduction of particular laws; it follows only that ... everyone be able to work up from this passive status to an active status (*Justice*, 256, 315; Ladd, 65, 80).

But surely this misses the point entirely. A formal possibility of participation is not the same as a real possibility. How, for example, does one 'work up' from being a woman in Italy? How does one 'work up' from being a black man in America? There is an important moral worry here and it is one which, quite frankly, Kant did not appreciate. It is a worry which was put most eloquently by William Ellery Channing in the following way:

> Our greatest error as a people is that we put an idolatrous trust in free institutions; as if these, by some major power, must secure our rights, however we enslave ourselves to evil passions. We need to learn that the forms of liberty are not its essence; that whilst the letter of a free constitution is preserved,

its spirit may be lost; that even its wisest provisions and most guarded powers may be made weapons of tyranny. In a country called free, a majority may become a faction, and a proscribed minority may be insulted, robbed and oppressed (*Works* (1853) II 255 ff.)

So let us admit that Kant's theory gives at most one side of the issues of political and social ethics. This is not really to condemn Kant, because it was only after the growth of the social sciences that we came into a position to realise just how great could be the gap between formal rights and actual *de facto* participation. One of the most painful things that thoughtful Americans are just now realising, for example, is how little the extension of legal rights to black people frees them from the oppression of racism. So Kant, in addressing himself to those moral evils in society which are susceptible to a purely legal cure, is addressing himself to a vital part of social ethics. But he is not, let us admit, covering the field in its entire scope. He leaves much work yet to be done by Marx and the nineteenth-century social theorists.

Acknowledging, then, that Kant is a typical Enlightenment figure in seeing the question 'How does one justify government?' as essentially equivalent to 'How does one justify a Rule of Law?', we can see that Kant does have an extremely plausible answer to this limited question. Law provides a non-violent way for the binding resolution of certain kinds of conflicts, and as an alternative to injustice and not merely disutility, it is morally obligatory on people to have such a rule:

Do no one an injustice (*neminem laede*), even if on this account you should have to stop associating with others and to avoid society altogether. If you cannot avoid [society], enter into a society with others in which each person can get and keep what is his own (*suum cuique tribue*). If the original formula is translated literally as 'give to each what is his own', it would be nonsense, inasmuch as one cannot give

132

to someone something that he already has. In order to make sense of this formula, it must be interpreted to mean: 'Enter into a condition under which what is his own is guaranteed to each person against everyone else' (*lex justitiae*) (*Justice*, 236; Ladd, 42).[16]

Given that this is a good justification for civil government and its Rule of Law, what *form* ought such government to take? That is, should it be absolutistic or representative? Kant, though vague about what he means by 'representative government', quite clearly comes down in its favour for two reasons. First, it is the form of government that would be rational for people to adopt in an antecedent position of choice. Since it is the very purpose of government to get claims fairly heard and resolved, each man in a state of nature would rationally want to adopt institutions in which his voice would be efficacious and thus opt for representative over absolutistic institutions. Second, there is Kant's view, which I shall discuss in more detail later, that the avoiding of war between civil communities is a fundamental duty of justice. International violence undermines domestic justice and thus must be avoided. Thus, because individual interest is so adversely affected by war, representative governments are less likely to wage war than totalitarian governments and so are to be preferred. As a sociological or historical generalisation this had doubtful credentials, but it would presumably be true if people did base such decisions solely on rational considerations. And so it does fit in with Kant's pattern of moral justification:[17]

The [republican] constitution is the only enduring political constitution in which the law is autonomous and is not annexed to any particular person. It is the ultimate end of all public Law and the only condition under which each person receives his due peremptorily (*Justice*, 341; Ladd, 112).

The republican constitution, besides the purity of

133

its origin (having sprung from the pure source of the concept of law), also gives a favourable prospect for the desired consequence, i.e. perpetual peace. The reason is this: if the consent of the citizens is required in order to decide that war should be declared ... nothing is more natural than that they should be very cautious in commencing such a poor game, decreeing for themselves all the calamities of war (*Perpetual Peace*, 351; Beck, 94).

Now though Kant is prepared to allow a very wide range of governments to count as republican or representative, such governments must all be based (in some rather special sense) on *consent*. This is not the explicit consent found in some social contract theory, but is to be explicated in terms of Kant's basic model of rational decision. A government can be said to be one of consent if it could have been chosen by a group of rational beings as a fair way of resolving their conflicts. This is plausible enough, though it does involve a certain circularity. Is it rational to choose representative government or is representative government simply whatever government it is rational to choose? It is not clear whether the notion of rational choice *justifies* representative government or explains the meaning of 'representative government'. Kant toys with both.

However, whether the claim that representative government is rational is or is not tautological, its truth gives Kant a way of elaborating a subtle theory of political obligation – that is, a theory explaining why we have a moral obligation to obey the law as such, a moral obligation to honour our legal obligations. We are morally obligated to obey the law, Kant claims, because we have, in the requisite sense, *consented* to it:

(One) juridical attribute inseparably bound up with the nature of a citizen as such ... is the lawful freedom to obey no law other than one to which he has given his consent.

134

A citizen must always be regarded as a colegislative member of the state (that is, not merely as a means, but at the same time as an end in himself), and as such he must give his free consent through his representatives, not only to the waging of war in general, but also to any particular declaration of war. It is only upon this limiting condition that the state may demand and dispose of a citizen's services if they involve being exposed to danger (*Justice*, 314, 345; Ladd, 78, 118).

By 'consent' here Kant means several things. First, in the sense already elaborated, he means that we consent to a government if it could have been rationally agreed to in an antecedent position of choice. (This is a negative test of justice.) He appears to use a second sense of 'consent', however, which is very like Locke's notion of *tacit* consent. We consent to a government by accepting its benefits and, as these benefits are possible only as a result of sacrifice by others, it is only fair that we make sacrifices (and obedience is a sacrifice) when our turn comes. For the harmony that law makes possible is a result of mutual forbearances on the part of citizens.

The basic idea here is that political obligation is essentially one of *reciprocity*.[18] A less technical name for this obligation is simply 'fair play'. Law and government form a system of social benefits which is made possible only as a result of mutual forbearances. The benefits I enjoy are possible only as a result of obedience by others. Therefore it is an obligation of reciprocity (since it is only fair) that I bear the necessary burden of obedience when my turn comes. I expect others to obey laws of which they do not approve; and so, if the laws are enacted according to the agreed procedure, it is only fair that I do likewise. Such reciprocity is required to make law and government possible. For as Kant reminds us in a remark I have already quoted, 'no one is bound to refrain from encroaching upon the possession of another man if the latter does not in equal measure guarantee that the same kind of restraint will be exercised with regard to him'. To exempt myself from rules which I rely on others to obey would be an act of injustice, for it would involve my claiming a greater freedom than I could rationally extend to others. Law is a social decision procedure and, having participated in and benefited from such a procedure, it is incoherent to claim a right to opt out when the going gets rough for me. (Even if I should feel it justified to opt out for moral reasons, it would be odd for me to claim this as a *right*.)

In addition to a literal notion of consent (i.e. my own agreement or that of my legislative representative), Kant seems to be operating with two technical notions. One consents to a system that one could have rationally adopted in a position of antecedent choice. And one consents, by a principle of fairness, by the fact of participation in a system of benefits based on reciprocal sacrifice.

With so many notions of consent floating around, the reader might suspect that it would be hard to find *any* government which was not, in some sense, a government of consent. This would lead one to suspect that Kant's defence of consent as required for obligation is merely so much liberal-bourgeois rhetoric – devoid of substance. And these suspicions are not, alas, unfounded. For this theory of political obligation brings us to one of the most controversial parts of Kant's general theory – his belief that the moral obligation to obey the law is not merely *prima facie* but is total or absolute under all possible circumstances. We are *never* (and Kant is quite explicit in this) morally justified in revolution or resistance. And so we must determine to what extent this rather reactionary view is merely a personal moral judgment on Kant's part and to what extent it is really a consequence of his theory.

Resistance and Revolution

Whatever one's own view about the justification of revolution, it must be admitted that Kant has one of the most subtle objections to its permissibility that has ever been formulated. He does not, like some political conservatives, appeal to the intrinsic wisdom of tradition and the done thing over change. Neither does he, like the Fascist, appeal to the State as an organic entity having a value over and above the values of its individual members. Rather his argument is based, as one might suspect, on an appeal to considerations of justice. I may not claim a moral right to do anything if I am not prepared (as a rational man) to extend to others the right to act in a similar fashion in similar circumstances. And since I could not regard it as justified for Jones to attempt the violent overthrow of my government merely because (for a variety of possible reasons) he detested it, I can claim no such right for myself. The revolutionary is in logically the same position as the vigilante who would punish in the state of nature and so acts immorally for the same reason. He is using coercion without an appeal to the kind of authoritative procedures which alone can justify its use:

> It is the people's duty to endure even the most intolerable abuse of supreme authority. The reason for this is that resistance to the supreme legislation can itself only be unlawful; indeed it must be conceived as destroying the entire lawful constitution, because, in order for it to be authorised, there would have to be a public law that would pemit the resistance. That is, the supreme legislation would have to contain a stipulation that it is not supreme and that in one and the same judgment the people as subjects should be made sovereign over him to whom they are subject; this is self-contradictory. The self-contradiction involved here is immediately evident if we ask who would act as judge in this controversy between the people and sovereign (because, juridically, they are still two distinct moral persons). (In such a controversy) it is plain that the people want to act as judge of their own cause (and that is absurd) (*Justice*, 320; Ladd, 86).

Though Kant's point is generally clear, there is some confusion here. At times, Kant seems to be making the point that it is incoherent to claim that there is a *legal* right to revolution. But, of course, this is non-controversial. The issue is whether there is a *moral* right. And Kant's argument here is that, since revolutions are violent and coercive and since coercion is justified only in a fair social practice, revolutions necessarily are not justified. The revolutionary, as his own judge and executioner, is not essentially different from the vigilante. The activities of the revolutionary, like those of the vigilante, may sometimes have good consequences, but they cannot be claimed as *rights*. So Kant sees disobedience to government as a form of violence and can thus apply his general argument against the injustice of non-institutionalised coercion to condemn it.

There is, however, another and more important confusion in Kant's account. For he does not distinguish between revolution and resistance. Revolution is a violent activity and thus may stand condemned by Kant's principles. However, there are forms of resistance (e.g. passive disobedience) which cannot, except in a Pickwickian sense, be construed as violent. And so it is hard to see how Kant's theory holds against resistance in this form. For merely refusing to obey a law is quite a different thing from banding together with a group of guerrillas and, perhaps after killing a great many people, setting up a new government. The argument Kant uses to condemn the latter cannot be generalised to condemn the former. At one time Kant almost seems to admit this, when he says, at *Justice*, 322 (Ladd, 89), that certain kinds of 'negative resistance' may be justified.[19]

So though I am willing to admit that Kant has presented a good (though perhaps not sufficient) case against violent revolution, he would have to show much more to make this case hold against non-violent resistance. Indeed, my own view is that a Kantian theory may be formulated for the *defence* of non-violent resistance under certain circumstances. For if our obligation to government is based, as Kant repeatedly

138

argues it is based, on the rational preferability of just over unjust procedures, then it would seem that a government's moral claim on the obedience of its citizens disappears when that government begins to control its citizens in an unjust fashion – through a purely arbitrary exercise of power rather than through just rules and fair procedures. For the obligation to obey the law, remember, is one of reciprocity – my obedience traded against the obedience of others *including government*. If government ignores its own legal limitations,[20] and abandons control through the Rule of Law, it becomes a merely *de facto* exercise of power and can, I think, properly be resisted. One could have made such a case, for example, against the government of Nazi Germany. Such a case is obviously not made out by an appeal to utility but rather rests on considerations of justice or fairness that are quite Kantian in character. Even so restricted a conception of justified resistance, however, was more than Kant in fact explicitly allowed.[21]

Now before closing my account of Kant's political theory, three final problems must be discussed. First, we need to examine Kant's much scorned 'retributive' theory of criminal punishment. Second, we need to understand Kant's views on such non-protective legislation as social welfare. Kant, like most Enlightenment liberals, views law as having primarily a negative function – protecting freedom against interference. But surely some government programmes which most of us regard as morally justified do not easily lend themselves to such a defence. Taxation for support of the poor, for example, does not initially appear to be the kind of coercion that can be justified by the doctrine of the moral title. Rather it seems that such laws reveal a positive function for government and its coercive machinery. So Kant must either condemn such laws, or show that they really do protect freedom in some non-apparent way, or develop some entirely new principle for their justification. Finally, we need to consider Kant's views, primarily as expressed in *Perpetual Peace*, on the nature and justification for world government and international law. For in the common

139

condemnation of Kant for his reactionary views on revolution and criminal punishment, it is often forgotten that his writings on world government reveal him as one of the most progressive and morally imaginative thinkers of his age.

The Nature and Justification of Criminal Punishment

Kant, as we have already seen, maintains that guilt is a necessary condition for the legitimate infliction of punishment. Intentionally to punish an innocent man, no matter how good the consequences of so doing, is a conceptual and a moral pathology. To punish an innocent man in the mistaken belief that he is guilty is a danger that we must carefully guard against. It is largely to avoid this danger that Kant inveighs against private revenge, vigilante activities and any other arrangement which allows a disputant to judge his own case and punish according to his (probably) biased decision. Criminal punishment is coercive power in its most brutal form, and thus it is absolutely essential that it be administered only under those procedures of due process found in a just Rule of Law. Such procedures, by securing fairness to the individual, often interfere with the goals of crime control and criminal rehabilitation. And thus the procedures may be condemned as disutilitarian (note the harsh criticism of recent United States Supreme Court decisions); but this, Kant argues, is the price we must pay if we are to have justice:

> Judicial punishment can never be used *merely* as a means to promote some other good for the criminal himself or for civil society, but instead it must in all cases be imposed on him only on the ground that he has committed a crime; for a human being can never be manipulated *merely* as a means to the purposes of someone else.... He must first be found to be deserving of punishment before any consideration is given to the utility of this punishment for himself or for his fellow citizens (*Justice*, 331; Ladd,

140

100. I have italicised the word 'merely' to point out that Kant is not committed in principle to opposing such *additional* goals as rehabilitation for a man being justly punished.)

That guilt is a necessary condition for legitimate infliction of criminal punishment will be accepted by most people – even, I should suppose, by all but the most fanatical utilitarians.[22] What will not be so readily accepted, however, is Kant's belief that guilt is a *sufficient* condition for punishment, regardless of utility. The famous and much scorned passage is worth quoting:

> Even if a civil society were to dissolve itself by common agreement of all its members (for example, if the people inhabiting an island decided to separate and disperse themselves around the world), the last murderer remaining in prison must be executed, so that everyone will duly receive what his actions are worth and so that the bloodguilt thereof will not be fixed on the people because they failed to insist on carrying out the punishment; for if they fail to do so, they may be regarded as accomplices in this public violation of legal justice (*Justice*, 333; Ladd, 102).

Kant here clearly holds a strong *retributive* theory of punishment, i.e. he holds that guilt *merits*, and is thus a sufficient condition for, the infliction of punishment. And this is the claim that is universally condemned – particularly by utilitarians – as primitive, unenlightened and barbaric.

But why is it so condemned? Typically, the charge is that infliction of punishment in such circumstances is pointless vengeance. But what is meant by the claim that the activity in question is pointless? If 'pointless' is to be analysed as 'disutilitarian', then the whole question is being begged. You cannot refute a retributive theory merely by noting that it is a retributive theory and not a utilitarian theory. The circle here is not large enough even to be interesting.

141

Why, then, might someone claim that guilt merits punishment? Such a claim might be made for either of two reasons: (1) Someone might maintain that the claim is a primitive and unanalysed proposition which is morally ultimate. Every ethical theory necessarily involves at least one such claim (e.g. 'happiness is good' or 'freedom is to be respected'), and the retributivist may be offering this as his candidate. Ethical argument has to terminate at some basic premise, and the retributivist may regard the 'fittingness' of guilt and suffering as basic in this way. (2) It might be maintained that the retributivist claim is demanded by a general theory of political obligation which is more plausible than any alternative theory. Such a theory will typically provide a technical *analysis* of such notions as crime and punishment and will thus not regard the retributivist claim as an indisputable primitive. It will be argued for as a kind of theorem within the system.

Claims of the first sort are, for obvious reasons, very difficult to evaluate. Thus it is fortunate that Kant's claim is of the second sort; he does not opt for the justice of retribution as a bit of intuitive moral knowledge. Rather, as we might expect, Kant offers a theory of punishment which is based on his general view that political obligation is to be analysed in terms of *reciprocity*. If the law is to remain just, it is important to guarantee that those who disobey it will not gain an unfair advantage over those who do obey voluntarily. Criminal punishment attempts to guarantee this, and, in its retribution, it attempts to restore the proper balance between benefit and obedience. The criminal himself has no complaint, because he has rationally willed or consented to his own punishment. That is, those very rules which he has broken work, when they are obeyed by others, to his own advantage as a *citizen*. He would have chosen such rules for himself in an antecedent position of choice. And since he derives benefit from them, he owes obedience as a *debt* to his fellow-citizens for their sacrifices in maintaining them. If he chooses not to sacrifice by exercising self-restraint and obedience, this is tantamount to his choosing to sacrifice in another way – namely, by paying the prescribed penalty:

> A transgression of the public law that makes him who commits it unfit to be a citizen is called ... a crime.... What kind and what degree of punishment does public legal justice adopt as its principle and standard? None other than the principle of equality (illustrated by the pointer of the scales of justice), that is, the principle of not treating one side more favourably than the other. Accordingly, any undeserved evil that you inflict on someone else among the people is one you do to yourself. If you vilify him, you vilify yourself; if you steal from him, you steal from yourself; if you kill him, you kill yourself.[23]

> To say, 'I will to be punished if I murder someone', can mean nothing more than, 'I submit myself along with everyone else to those laws which, if there are any criminals among the people, will naturally include penal laws' (*Justice*, 331, 332, 335; Ladd, 99, 101, 105).[24]

This analysis of punishment regards it as a *debt* owed to the law-abiding members of one's community; and, once paid, it allows re-entry into the community of good citizens on equal status.

Now there is much, of course, that can still be said against this analysis. For one thing, the view of the criminal as one who does not deserve a place in the community necessarily involves a certain amount of moral pretension. It neglects Bishop Creighton's reminder that 'the good are not so good as they think themselves; the wicked are not so bad as the good think them'. How many of the law-abiding, for example, have that status because of fear of punishment or lack of opportunity rather than because they are restrained by morally creditable motives? And how many of these same people, though adhering to the letter of the law, violate it in spirit and thereby undermine (in a manner safe from punishment) the value of their community? Just as the utilitarian often undermoralises the practice of punishment, so the retributivist tends to overmoralise it, investing it with a moral righteousness that is, at least in part, pretence.

However, in spite of its weaknesses, Kant's retributivism does rest upon an analytical theory. It is not merely the piece of vindictive and primitive emotionalism that it has often been portrayed to be by many of its critics.

The Common Good

Kant, it will be recalled, attempts in theory to limit the sphere of political ethics (the proper objects for governmental coercion) to perfect duties to others. Since such activities as murder and breach of contract quite clearly do violate perfect duties to others, they are clearly to be regarded as proper objects of State coercion. But what about the aid of those, like the poor, in social distress? Our duties to help them, according to Kant, are imperfect. Non-benevolence, though not consistently willable as a law of nature, is possible as a law of nature because it does not involve any interference with the freedom of those who are disadvantaged. It is morally good to help such people, but it is not obligatory in the strong sense required to justify governmental coercion. For it is only when freedom is violated, according to Kant, that legal interference with people is justified. Given his general theory, then, one would expect that Kant would come out in strong condemnation of social welfare, arguing that it is unjust to tax Jones in order to be benevolent to Smith. At the very least, one would expect Kant to regard welfare programmes as a good quality of government but not as one of government's fundamental obligations. Such expectations are surprised, however, in the *Rechtslehre*:

The general Will of the people has united itself into

a society in order to maintain itself continually, and for this purpose it has subjected itself to the internal authority of the state in order to support those members of the society who are not able to support themselves. Therefore, it follows from the nature of the state that the government is authorised to require the wealthy to provide the means of sustenance to those who are unable to provide the most necessary needs of nature for themselves. Because their existence depends on the act of subjecting themselves to the commonwealth for the protection and care required in order to stay alive, they have bound themselves to contribute to the support of their fellow-citizens, and this is the ground for the state's right to require them to do so (*Justice*, 326; Ladd, 93).

Now though we may applaud this rare instance of benevolence on Kant's part, it is by no means clear that this view is consistent with his general theory. Here he simply asserts, without substantial argument, that government has the right – indeed the obligation – to tax for public welfare. Kant's claim that the wealthy submit to government for the protection and care which allows them to stay alive can surely not defend a duty of positive benevolence, for this care and protection in question is purely negative – the removal of obstacles to freedom. So it is very difficult to see what Kant is up to.

What seems to be the case is that Kant, primarily interested in government as a just protector of rights, simply did not give the positive powers of government much thought. All that he says in the short passage on public welfare in the *Rechtslehre* has the character of being quite perfunctory. However, one can make out a case for some public welfare along Kantian lines, and I should suggest what follows as such a provisional account.

Kant uses the notion of benevolence quite ambiguously. He sometimes means by this duty the duty to make another's ends my own and positively promote his happiness. As such, it seems to me plausible to say that such benevolence, if it is a duty at all, is imperfect

in character and thus not a proper object of State coercion. However, he sometimes means by benevolence
something considerably more restricted: helping
others in distress. Now such actions are, I think, proper
objects of such minimal State coercion as taxation because, in at least one sense, they can be construed as
perfect duties.[25] They rest on the innate right of *freedom* in each person. Certain kinds of social and economic disadvantage inhibit, in quite a literal sense,
the freedom of those who are disadvantaged. Those
who have to concentrate (because of a lack of such
basic needs as food and clothing and shelter) on mere
animal survival are barred from the realisation of any
of their uniquely human potentials. They have obstacles in the way of their freedom to such an extent
that they are more things than persons. To the extent
that these obstacles are removable by human agency,
then, it may plausibly be regarded as a perfect duty to
remove them. This duty, grounded in the value of
freedom, is very like the doctrine of the moral title –
both in function and derivation. Kant himself failed
to develop such an argument, I think, because he
never in his own mind clearly distinguished positive
benevolence from relief of distress. Of course, the distinction is one of degree, and reasonable men can
differ about where to draw the line between meri-
torious benevolence and dutiful relief. But the distinction holds in principle, and the existence of borderline
cases does not establish that there are no clear cases.
We may disagree, for example, over whether the absence of any means of transportation inhibits in a
morally relevant way the freedom of the man so disadvantaged. But surely we know that disease and
hunger do so inhibit and that failure to own a private
aircraft does not so inhibit. Thus, within a consistent
Kantian framework, a case for limited social welfare
can be made out – even though Kant did not himself
succeed in making it out.[26]

I should like to close this discussion of Kant's political ethics with a brief discussion of his essay *Perpetual Peace*, a defence of world government which elaborates some of the ideas sketched in the *Rechtslehre*. Since it is perhaps the clearest and most elegant of all Kant's writings, there is no point in summarising it in detail. Rather I simply want to indicate its general direction and importance.

Quite generally, the essay is devoted to two topics: a defence of the moral necessity for world government (of a federal form) and a set of maxims for present governments to follow so as to make world government more likely. He argues, for example, that governments should be representative because governments so constituted are less likely to make war – war being the greatest enemy of an international Rule of Law. Also, he argues that governments which do conduct wars should not conduct them in ways so oppressive and cruel as to make eventual harmony among nations difficult to attain.

More important than these practical maxims, however, is his defence for the moral necessity for some kind of world federation. Governments, he argues, can be viewed as moral persons. As such, they quite literally stand to each other in the same way that classical social contract theory imagined individuals to stand to each other in the state of nature. They have perpetual conflicts in the absence of any fair or just way to resolve these conflicts. And though governments righteously go to war and speak of punishing other nations for wrongdoing, this is simply rhetoric. Such national action is simply vigilante activity writ large, for it is devoid of justice.

What is in fact the case is that governments typically wage war for their own advantage and thus, quite unjustly, sacrifice others for their own self-interest. Or even if they interfere for the supposed good of the others (to defend 'democracy' or some such thing), this is a moral analogue to imperialism which represents just that kind of paternalism which any true defender

147

of freedom would want to oppose. Certain acts of national self-defence are excusable, but even these rest on no principle of justice – for where is the due process, the decision procedure with authority, which would distinguish a felt wrong from a real wrong? We all know of many nations which have fought wars of so-called self-defence which were simply responses to wounded national honour. National states present a paradigm of the pathology that develops when parties to a controversy act as judges with respect to their own claims of right. (Even when a war has a morally good outcome, it is generally not very plausible to argue that the victor had a *right* to engage in it.)

Thus, because of the variability of individual and national judgment (a variability made more likely because of the hysteria that surrounds war), the international climate is more one of rationalisation than reason – moral rhetoric rather than moral practice. And, as such, it presents a pathology which is, writ large, the pathology of the state of nature between individuals. And thus world government can be regarded as the only legitimate cure for this pathology – the only cure compatible with justice. Perpetual peace, then, is the fundamental political duty. For all that is morally valuable rests on the freedom of the individual human being. His freedom can be secured only in just civil society, and civil society can be secured only in a world of peace under just law. The advice of this sane man, then, speaks to us today as much as it spoke to his contemporaries:

> Now, moral-practical reason within us voices its irresistible veto: *There shall be no war*, either between thee and me in a state of nature or among states, which are still in a lawless condition in their external relations with one another, even though internally they are not.... As a matter of fact, it can be said that the establishment of a universal and enduring peace is not just a part, but rather constitutes the whole, of the ultimate purpose of Law within the bounds of pure reason.... This Idea should be attempted and carried out through

gradual reform according to fixed principles. Only in this way is it possible to approach continually closer to the highest political good – perpetual peace (*Justice*, 344–5; Ladd, 128–9).

Appendix

A Note on Kant's Influence

It would be hard to overestimate the influence of Kant's philosophy. However, given the many different and often competing facets of Kant's thought, it is not too surprising that this influence has expressed itself in a variety of diverse and often competing philosophical movements, some attempting to apply Kant's views and others attempting to refute them. Such philosophical movements as Absolute Idealism, Positivism, Pragmatism and Existentialism have all owed something to Kant. It has been truly said that one may philosophise for or against Kant, but one may not philosophise without him.

If one stresses Kant's notion that the mind makes an active contribution to knowledge, and plays down Kant's claim that this formal contribution operates on a *given* matter, then some form of Idealism is the natural outcome. Kant maintained that his theory was solely an account of *phenomena*; but he also claimed (admittedly for no very good reason) that there was a world of noumenal 'things in themselves' lying behind these phenomena. This was, given man's cognitive faculties, an unknowable world – an object for faith alone. When later philosophers (e.g. Fichte) realised how weak were the arguments for the *Ding an sich*, they dispensed with the noumenal world entirely, and thus the road was open for Absolute Idealism – the claim that 'everything is mind'. Hegel's later Absolute Idealism, in so far as it rests on a denial of the form–content distinction, is intelligible only if one understands it as in part a revolt against a Kantian dichotomy.

If Absolute Idealism originally arose as a criticism of

Kant, it did not remain so limited for long. It developed into a full-blown metaphysical school that gloried in quasi-mystical speculative claims that far transcended the rather modest nonsense indulged in by the pre-Kantian rationalists. Quite naturally later Idealism encouraged an intensely anti-metaphysical reaction – Logical Empiricism or Positivism. These philosophers viewed proper philosophy as a *therapeutic* enterprise, the goal of which was to cure the metaphysical 'disease'. Not without good reason, some early Positivists (e.g. the early Wittgenstein) recalled a previous anti-metaphysician and paid him due respect. They did this by attempting to formulate a principle of meaning or significance (the empirical verifiability criterion) which allowed them to reach (to no one's surprise) a remarkably Kantian conclusion – namely, that speculative metaphysical claims are not just false but *meaningless*. Other positivists (e.g. Carnap) recalled Kant's synthetic *a priori* and were thus somewhat less enchanted with him.

In ethics, Kant's stress on freedom or autonomy as the essential feature of human personality contributed to such diverse forms of philosophical voluntarism as Pragmatism (Peirce, James and C. I. Lewis) and Existentialism (Kierkegaard). In political philosophy, Kant has always strongly influenced those liberals (in the classical sense) who seek to defend freedom on principle. F. A. von Hayek's *The Constitution of Liberty* (Chicago, 1960) is a remarkably Kantian book, and his forthcoming *Law, Liberty and Legislation* (which I have seen in manuscript) is even more so. I have already noted in the text the extent of Kant's influence on such contemporary writers in normative ethics as John Rawls and H. L. A. Hart.

But what about Kant as a *transcendental* philosopher? In the text I stressed that Kant's central contribution was to be found in his attempt to discover the presuppositions that render knowledge possible and experience intelligible. As it happens, this uniquely Kantian conception of philosophy informs some of the most exciting and creative philosophical work currently being undertaken. Particularly important in this regard are P. F. Strawson's *Individuals, An Essay in Descriptive Metaphysics* (London, 1959), Sydney Shoemaker's *Self-Knowledge and Self-Identity* (Ithaca, 1963) and Stuart Hampshire's *Thought and Action* (London, 1959). Not only is this work important; it is highly controversial.[1]

Kant was the greatest philosopher of his age and wrote extensively on most of the primary problems of philosophy. That his work is still highly relevant should thus surprise no one.[2]

Notes

Preface

1 'Kant's Concept of a Right Action', *The Monist*, vol. 51, no. 4 (Oct. 1967) 574–98. For a criticism of the argument of this article, see Peter Laska's 'Kant on Moral Worth', *Kant-Studien*, 59 Jahrgang, Heft 3 (1968) 374–83.

Chapter 1

1 In my treatment of the development of ·Kant's thought, I have leaned heavily on the excellent discussion in the first chapter of Robert Paul Wolff's *Kant's Theory of Mental Activity* (Cambridge, Mass., 1963).
2 Consider the following as one example of how rules can order experience: One can slide into a bag of sand as often as one wishes, but it is only in a context governed by the rules of baseball that such behaviour can constitute the act of sliding into second base.
3 See, for example, 5.6, 5.61, 5.62 and 6.362. For an interesting discussion of the Kantian character of Wittgenstein's thought in the *Tractatus*, see chap. xi of Erik Stenius, *Wittgenstein's Tractatus* (Oxford, 1960). Later, in the first *Critique*, Kant moves from idealism to phenomenalism. There he will claim that the 'matter' of knowledge is not mind-dependent but is *given*.
4 *Kant: Philosophical Correspondence, 1759–99*, translated and edited by Arnulf Zweig (Chicago, 1967) p. 72.
5 One might define events as caused happenings and thereby attempt to make the principle analytic. But then, of course, we would want to raise the following question: Must every happening have a cause?

6   I have drawn the story about the car from W. H. Walsh's useful article 'Categories', *Kant-Studien* (1953–4).

7   For example: We all know that there are substances in the world – that is, objects which continue in existence when unperceived. But if we allow ourselves to become persuaded by Hume, we shall begin to have creeping (almost neurotic) doubts about this. Surely, Hume argues, all that I am *really* certain about are my present sensations or 'impressions'. After all, we are sometimes mistaken in our claims about objects, but never in our claims about present sensations. So how do we really know if we are *ever* correct in our judgments about external objects? To be seduced by this passage from 'am sometimes mistaken' to 'might always be mistaken' (an argument almost definitive of empiricist scepticism) is to be put into the position of believing that to claim anything stronger than 'red patch there now' is to be intellectually disreputable.

8   Remember that 'contributed by Reason' is not (at least when Kant is at his best) to be read as a psychological claim. Rather it should be unpacked in the following way: A principle is to be regarded as a contribution of Reason if (i) it is an essential part of our knowledge and (ii) it cannot be analysed empirically – that is, its meaning cannot be explicated solely in terms of contingent association among sensory data. Kant writes in the rationalist tradition of innate ideas, but it is a mistake to regard this tradition as one postulating occult mental entities. It rather involves a theory about how certain claims are to be analysed. (On this, see Noam Chomsky, *Cartesian Linguistics* (New York, 1966).) In the discussion which follows, I shall illustrate Kant's position by considering his argument (against Hume) that the causal maxim is a contribution of Reason because it satisfies these two conditions.

9   For more on this point, see Lewis White Beck, 'Can Kant's Synthetic Judgments be Made Analytic?', in *Studies in the Philosophy of Kant* (Indianapolis, 1965).

10   For the details of this explication of the argument of the Second Analogy as an answer to Hume, see

Lewis White Beck, 'Once More Unto the Breach', *Ratio* (1967). Though I believe that Beck has indeed isolated Kant's answer to Hume, I do not share his view that the answer is a success. See my 'Kant's Second Analogy as an Answer to Hume', *Ratio*, June 1969. See also P. F. Strawson, *The Bounds of Sense* (London, 1966) pp. 133–46.

11 Kant is famous for claiming that he denied knowledge of metaphysical entities like God to make room for faith in them. This, however, strikes me as a lame remark and as not consistent with the best insights of the *Critique*. For given the radical character of Kant's objection to metaphysical claims, faith is no better off than knowledge. For if a proposition P is incoherent or meaningless by transcending the bounds of its intelligible use, then in having faith in P I no more have an idea what I am having faith in than I would have an idea what I would be claiming in claiming to know that P.

12 P. F. Strawson has made a similar kind of point. He asks that we consider the sentence 'The present king of France is wise' as uttered in a time, like the present, when there is no king of France. The sentence is non-contradictory and grammatically well formed and thus appears to have a sense. But this appearance is an illusion, as can be seen by considering whether the 'claim' being made is true or false. The temptation is to believe that, since there is no king, the claim is false. But, by the law of excluded middle, this would entail that the claim 'It is not the case that the present king of France is wise' is true. However, the failure of the subject term to refer is what tempted us to reject the initial claim as false, and thus it would appear that this latter claim is false too. Not wishing to abandon the law of excluded middle, we must realise that the claim is neither true nor false but is rather a pseudo-claim without sense. This is because a presupposition of the intelligible use of descriptive claims has been violated – the presupposition that their subject terms do in fact refer. What, for example, would you make of Jones who, knowing full well that you have no daughter, soberly inquired after the health of your daugh-

ter? Surely you would take him to be talking nonsense. Neither 'She's fine' nor 'She's not fine' would tempt you as answers. Strawson's point about the conditions for intelligible use of language in certain contexts explains a special kind of nonsense (very like Kant's transcendental illusion) with a notion of 'presupposition' that is very helpful in elucidating Kant's similar notion ('On Referring', *Mind* (1950)).

13 For an elaboration of this point, see John Rawls's article 'Justice as Fairness', in *Philosophy, Politics and Society, Second Series,* ed. Peter Laslett and W. G. Runciman (Oxford, 1964). Of all current writers in normative ethics, Rawls seems to me the most Kantian in spirit.

14 Note the contrast with John Stuart Mill: 'Despotism is a legitimate mode of government in dealing with barbarians, provided the end be their improvement and the means justified by actually effecting that end' (*On Liberty,* Introduction).

15 It is also, of course, *unfair* to blame or punish those whose actions are not free.

16 This as stated is, of course, an oversimplification. It is controversial, for example, whether reason explanations are reducible to causal explanations. Also, if my behaviour is explained by a reason that is unconscious, it is not clear that my act is free. An exploration of this topic, however, would take us far afield of the present inquiry. For a discussion of some of the issues involved, see the article 'Purpose and Teleology', *The Monist* (1968), by my colleague J. L. Cowan.

17 The utilitarian might attempt to counter in the following way: Though it is just a fact that people pursue their own happiness, it is not a fact that people pursue the happiness of all people equally; and it is this latter which utilitarianism enjoins. To this, however, the Kantian has the following reply: The happiness of everyone equally cannot be established as a value by a Mill-like empirical argument. Rather it will be argued for by a rational principle of justice, one which commands that qualitative identicals be not treated differently. It is *unfair* to place my own happiness above that of another, and fairness is not a utili-

tarian concept.

18   The concept of a fully rational being describes nothing to be met with in any possible experience. It is thus an Idea of Reason. Kant would therefore be guilty of transcendental illusion if he employed the concept as anything but a model.

19   The Categorical Imperative, Kant's supreme principle of morality, is a test for determining whether actions are morally permissible or impermissible. If an action is morally impermissible, we have a duty not to perform it. Kant sometimes refers to duties as categorical imperatives.

20   The most illuminating and detailed treatment of Kant's categorical–hypothetical distinction is to be found in Lewis White Beck, 'Apodictic Imperatives', in *Studies in the Philosophy of Kant*. It is important to realise, as Beck realises, that Kant is not saying that the value of ends is irrelevant in determining duty, only that their value is not a function of the degree to which they are desired. Failure to see this distinction is at the root of the common belief that Kant's theory is totally anti-teleological.

21   For a contemporary elaboration of this sort of argument, see H. L. A. Hart's remarkably Kantian article 'Are There Any Natural Rights?', *Philosophical Review* (1955). This is reprinted in Anthony Quinton's *Political Philosophy* (Oxford, 1967).

22   Unless, of course, I had (for example) *promised* to make Jones happy. But then the duty, like that created in a marriage, would be perfect. It is the interference with rights which makes an act a violation of perfect duty. All duties of contract are, therefore, perfect duties; but not all perfect duties are duties of contract. Kant also has two other ways of distinguishing perfect from imperfect duties: (1) Imperfect duties, unlike perfect duties, allow some latitude in the time and manner of their fulfilment. There are, for example, a variety of equally satisfactory ways of promoting the happiness of others. (2) Perfect duties are such that their contraries are not *possible* as laws of nature; imperfect duties are such that their contraries, though possible as laws of nature, could not be consistently

158

willed to be laws of nature. This is a way of distinguishing perfect from imperfect duties by reference to the *criteria* used in their determination. I shall have more to say about this later.

23 Had Kant had the misfortune to live through the twentieth century, his observation of totalitarian thought control might have prompted him to retract his optimism on this point. However, his argument could be reconstructed in the following way: The only worth of a disposition like love from the moral point of view depends upon its being freely adopted. Thus if the State makes me feel a certain emotion, the State has not thereby enforced a duty to self, since the duty is to adopt this disposition freely. Even if the State could enforce such duties, however, its attempts to do so would spell an end to individual liberty. For a detailed and illuminating discussion on this general topic, see Herbert Morris, 'Punishment for Thoughts', *The Monist* (1965).

24 I say 'may' here for the following reason: Interference with the happiness of others is not *per se* a breach of duty. If Sarah and Sophie both love me, then in choosing to marry Sarah I may make Sophie quite unhappy. It could hardly be said, however, that in so doing I have violated any of Sophie's rights (unless there is more to the story than I am telling).

Chapter 2

1 The use of 'right' as equivalent to 'morally permissible' deviates from ordinary usage in that it does not distinguish 'right' from 'all right'. This deviation is intentional. Though morally indifferent actions (those merely 'all right') are trivial and uninteresting if we *know* that they are indifferent, they can be very important if we do not know this — especially if we believe that they are morally wrong. Much sexual conduct, for example, is morally trivial, but people feel much unnecessary apprehension and guilt from not realising this. Thus it seems to me a real virtue of Kant's moral criterion that it is framed with a view, not merely to

159

duty for its own sake, but to moral indifference as well: 'According to categorical imperatives certain actions are *permissible* or *impermissible*, i.e. morally possible or impossible, while some of these actions or their contraries are morally necessary, i.e. obligatory' (*Metaphysics of Morals*, 220; Gregor, 20). A right action, then, is one which violates no categorical imperative or duty. One who values freedom will quite naturally be interested in sheltering such actions from interference – especially when this interference comes, as it often does, under the banners of righteousness.

2 A. R. C. Duncan, *Practical Reason and Morality* (London, 1957) pp. 28–32.

3 Stephen Toulmin, *The Place of Reason in Ethics* (Cambridge, 1958); Kurt Baier, *The Moral Point of View* (Ithaca, 1958); Marcus Singer, *Generalisation in Ethics* (New York, 1961); and R. M. Hare, *The Language of Morals* and *Freedom and Reason* (Oxford, 1952 and 1963).

4 These two major divisions in contemporary meta-ethics, and the leading exponents of each, are discussed in detail in William Frankena's 'Recent Conceptions of Morality', in *Morality and the Language of Conduct*, ed. Hector-Neri Castañeda and George Nakhnikian (Detroit, 1963).

5 Kant's contrast between the Ideal of pure moral philosophy and a material metaphysics of morals has an interesting analogue in game and decision theory. Such theories provide criteria of rational decision in certain kinds of choice situations for agents specified in a certain ideal way (e.g. as maximisers of individual utility). However, it is by no means clear that in particular cases the rational thing for a *human* to do is to act in the way the theory dictates, for he may have a variety of competing desires and obligations. Human beings are not in fact as simply constituted as are the theoretical agents employed in the model.

6 In chap. i of her *Laws of Freedom*, (Oxford, 1963), Mary J. Gregor presents a useful discussion of the pure–*a priori* distinction. Her work on Kant's material moral philosophy is the best that has appeared in English.

7 Hare, *The Language of Morals* and *Freedom and Reason*.

8 Alan Gewirth, 'Categorial Consistency in Ethics', *Philosophical Quarterly* (1967).

9 H. L. A. Hart, 'Legal and Moral Obligation', in *Essays in Moral Philosophy*, ed. A. I. Melden (Seattle, 1958).

10 These formulations occur (as imperatives) at *Foundations*, 421, 429 and 438 (Beck, 39, 47 and 57). Kant never expresses formulation (2) in terms of pure rationality itself but only in terms of humanity. But this is surely an oversight. For he believes that we must treat *all* rational beings (not just human beings) as ends and, indeed, that human beings deserve such treatment only because they are rational.

11 Note that this differs from the utilitarian demand that each man merits equal *consideration*. For equal consideration is compatible with great injustice. For example, I might give equal consideration to slaves in that I think that their happiness is to be computed on the same scale as the happiness of the slaveholders, but argue that the happiness of the latter (because there are more of them, say) *outweighs* the unhappiness of the former. This is exactly what Kant wants to preclude. It is immoral to deny the freedom of any man against his rational will, no matter how good (on balance) the consequences of so doing.

12 Kant's third formulation of the Categorical Imperative employs the notion of a 'kingdom of ends'. As I view this notion, it is meant to describe the moral community that would result if everyone did act on maxims which respected the dignity as ends in themselves of all rational beings. Our social world is not like this but, as a political ideal, it ought to be.

13 H. J. Paton, *The Categorical Imperative* (London, 1963) pp. 168–9.

14 If put somewhat more cautiously, there may be an important insight in Paton's claim. If a man is totally incapable of appreciating the relevance of moral considerations or is totally unmoved by them, then it is odd to regard him as a proper object of moral respect. Those with psychopathic personalities are hardly in a

position to demand treatment as ends in themselves. For more on this very complex moral issue, see Herbert Fingarette's 'Acceptance of Responsibility' in his *On Responsibility* (New York, 1967).

15 See William Frankena, *Ethics* (Englewood Cliffs, 1963) pp. 47–8.

16 Getting completely clear about these two doctrines of freedom would take a book in itself. For the best existing treatment, see Lewis White Beck, *A Commentary on Kant's Critique of Practical Reason* (Chicago, 1960) pp. 176 ff.

17 This will not mean that fully rational beings, since they do right by their own nature, have no dignity. These beings could act immorally if they had the inclination. It is constitutive of their nature, however, that they have no such inclinations. Thus the necessity of these beings to act morally does not mean that they are without freedom (*Willkür*) and thus without dignity. We might as well claim that a man who never has the inclination to steal has his freedom limited thereby.

18 By 'responsible' in this discussion, I mean more than 'causally related'. Even animals and material objects can be responsible in a purely causal sense, e.g. 'The slippery pavement was responsible for the accident.' A person is capable of being responsible in a stronger sense, however, in that he can, say, bring about harm through his own *fault*. To act with fault is to act with a mental state sufficient for culpability, e.g. to act purposely, knowingly or recklessly. Such a conception of fault is sometimes moral in character, but it does not have to be. It has a prominent place, for example, in *legal* conceptions of responsibility.

19 Recall the contrast I previously drew (Chapter 1) between reason explanations and causal explanations. Surely not all instances of the former will necessarily involve a conception of moral duty. Going into the bank because I want to cash a cheque is surely more like going in because I promised to meet someone inside than it is like going in because I was placed under post-hypnotic suggestion. And if one is free to the extent that one acts from reasons rather than causes,

then surely the range of free or responsible actions is broader than the class of actions motivated by duty. Kant often fails to see this and often seems to suggest that my action, if it does not involve the 'noumenal' dimension of duty, is *nothing but* a part of the phenomenal causal order. But this, as Kant himself realises on other occasions, is confused. Even my 'phenomenal' *actions* are to be distinguished from *happenings*.

Chapter 3

1 H. L. A. Hart, *The Concept of Law* (Oxford, 1961) p. 190.

2 For a detailed discussion of the functions (moral and epistemological) of the typic of judgment, see Beck, *Commentary*, pp. 154 ff.

3 The qualification 'at least *prima facie*' is needed here for the following reason: There are certain things which, though I would not desire them for myself, are morally permissible to impose on others. Criminal punishment is an example. Such punishment, since it goes against the wishes of the criminal in depriving him of his freedom is *prima facie* wrong – that is, it stands in need of an overriding moral justification. Its justification consists in that it is called for by a social practice or institution that serves the rational interests of everyone (even the criminal) as a citizen. The institution would have been chosen (even by the criminal) in some antecedent position of choice. Thus, in a rather technical sense, the criminal may be said to have willed his own punishment. (I shall have more to say about this in the final chapter.) Having adopted a social practice, we may have to do particular things which are undesired or are even *prima facie* wrong. If we were going to decide each case solely on its perceived merits, there would be no point in having social practices at all. For more on this see John Rawls, 'Two Concepts of Rules', *Philosophical Review* (1955), and my own 'Kalin on the Categorical Imperative', *Ethics* (1969).

4 Paton, *The Categorical Imperative*, p. 163.

5   For a discussion of this doctrine, see *Metaphysical Elements of Justice*, 230 ff. (Ladd, 35–40).

6   This is not an argument of enlightened egoism. That is, it is not being claimed that you ought to protect others because it is *probable* that you will need help some day and can thus cash in on a universal practice of protection. Rather it is claimed that *if* you were being attacked, you would desire assistance. You know this about yourself even if, in point of fact, you never let yourself get into a vulnerable position. And so it would be irrational to will universal non-protection, because in so doing you would be advocating treating another in a way you could not rationally will to be treated in similar circumstances. This argument is of the same form that Kant uses to establish the imperfect duty of benevolence (helping others in distress) at *Foundations*, 423 (Beck, 41).

7   Gregor, *Laws of Freedom*, p. 43.

8   Strictly speaking, ignoring a rape is an omission rather than an act. Since we may be morally culpable for such omissions, however, this distinction will be irrelevant for the purposes of this study.

9   See Gregor, *Laws of Freedom*, p. 187, and *Metaphysics of Morals*, 464 (Gregor, 134).

10   Every man has happiness and perfection as essential ends. However, *my own* perfection and the happiness of *others* are the only ends which are also duties. For I cannot make another perfect (though I can place *obstacles* to his perfection) and will, of necessity, seek my own happiness.

11   Robert Paul Wolff, *Journal of Philosophy*, vol. LXI, no. 7 (1964) 231–2 (a review of Gregor's *Laws of Freedom*).

12   It might seem that perfection cannot be an essential end unless men necessarily seek it. But, if men necessarily seek it, why does Kant say that cultivating our own perfection (unlike pursuing happiness) is a *duty*? The answer is that Kant's derivation of this imperfect duty is confused, for his argument involves the following paradox: The duty to seek my perfection can be derived only if I (in some sense) already desire my perfection. Otherwise there will be no contradic-

tion in my will if I decide to follow a course of non-perfection. The kind of contradiction in the will required for the objective derivation of an imperfect duty can arise only if it can be shown that, by ignoring this duty, I would be willing against one of my *necessary* ends.

13 There are, of course, immense problems with this position. We know that the discovery of necessary human ends is neither an empirical-scientific nor a moral inquiry, but Kant never tells us just what sort of an inquiry it is. Thus we do not know the ground rules for evaluating success or failure, and we are thus at an unfair disadvantage in attempting to evaluate Kant's conclusion that there are just two essential ends – happiness and perfection. Inquiries into the 'nature of man' are teleological. But if, as the critical philosophy teaches, such inquiries yield simply 'as if' conclusions, how can we be so confident in building our morality around them? One cannot help feeling that some important questions are being begged and that Kant thus shares some of the failures of traditional natural-law theory.

14 H. L. A. Hart, *Law, Liberty and Morality* (London, 1963) p. 46.

15 This may be illustrated by a consideration of promising. The liberty of breaking a promise cannot be extended to everyone, for the success of the practice of promising as an institution depends upon the general keeping of promises. As a practice, promising gives rise to patterns of legitimate expectations; but such expectations would clearly not be possible in a world where 'promises' were generally broken. This will not be sufficient to demonstrate the immorality of promise-breaking, however, unless the practice itself (like the Rule of Law, say) serves a moral function. (Monopoly could not succeed as a game unless its rules were generally followed; it is odd, however, to say that someone who breaks the rules of this trivial game is breaching a *moral* obligation.) And so the parasite argument will not alone be sufficient to establish the immorality of promise-breaking.

Two courses, then, remain open. First, one might

165

argue that having a promising institution functions to further a systematic harmony of human purposes. Second, one might point out that – regardless of the moral merits of the institution as a whole – participation in that institution (by promising) typically affects the interests and expectations of other people. It is (like a contract) a way of getting people to let down their guard and count on others in certain ways. Having entered into such a relationship with another person, it would be to treat him directly as a means to ignore the requirements of that relationship.

16   It should always be understood that the maxim of the action is to be specified with respect to relevant circumstances. It is not, for example, immoral for me to attend a concert tonight because, if everyone in the world tried to attend that concert tonight, the consequences would be world chaos. My maxim, then, will have to be something like this: 'Attend C at time t if C and t are such that not everyone wants to attend C at t.' If everyone does want to do this, of course, then some fair method of deciding position will have to be agreed to.

17   Sometimes, of course, it would be *logically* impossible to extend the liberty to all men, and then you would not need to consider consequences. This will happen when the action you seek to perform (like promising) gets its meaning only in the context of an ongoing social practice. Not all actions that Kant wants to prohibit, however, are such that their meaning is tied to such a practice. We have an obligation to protect freedom (by preventing its violation) and such protection is possible only in the context of a just Rule of Law. But this is a contingent and not a necessary truth, i.e. 'freedom' can be understood in independence from such a context.

Chapter 4

1   In this way, Kant's view differs rather sharply from Mill's in *On Liberty* which it superficially resembles. Mill tries to give a positive defence of freedom by

arguing (usually not very plausibly) that freedom leads to good utilitarian consequences. Kant regards such proceedings as doubtful and irrelevant. For the man who values freedom on principle is the man who defends it *in spite of* disutility. Surely no purely utilitarian considerations, for example, would justify allowing free speech to a racist organisation like the Ku Klux Klan, for their nonsense surely does much more harm than good. And neither is it clear that free *institutions* are best defended in a utilitarian fashion. It is not too hard to imagine (as Aldous Huxley did in *Brave New World*) a society of minimal freedom where happiness is still maintained. Thus Mill's position is really so much empirical guesswork. It is in part because of his desire to avoid this sort of thing that Kant attempts to establish the importance of freedom by a principle of justice.

2   For a contemporary elaboration of this notion of the social contract, see John Rawls, 'Justice as Fairness', in *Philosophy, Politics and Society, Second Series*. Rawls, like Kant, sees the contract as essentially a rational decision model for the co-operative adoption of social institutions.

3   'The only purpose for which power can rightfully be exercised over any member of a civilised community, against his will, is to prevent harm to others' (*On Liberty*, chap. i).

4   Mill can be interpreted in such a way as to make his view much closer to Kant's. See 'A Re-Reading of Mill on Liberty', in J. C. Rees, *Political Studies* (Oxford, 1960).

5   I am suggesting that a contrast between Locke and Kant will be of aid in understanding Kant's views. I am not suggesting that, as a matter of historical fact, Kant's *Rechtslehre* is written as an attack on Locke. The argument of the following section is condensed from my article 'A Paradox in Locke's Theory of Natural Rights', September *Dialogue* (1969). See also the section 'The Right of the State to Punish', in T. H. Green, *Works*, vol. 2: *Lectures on the Principles of Political Obligation* (London, 1890).

6   All references to Locke's *Second Treatise* are from

Peter Laslett's edition of *Two Treatises of Government* (Cambridge, 1960). All citations are followed by a number in parentheses indicating the paragraph from which the material was drawn. In quoting from Locke, I have taken some stylistic liberties in so far as these do not affect the sense. When I speak of 'natural rights' and 'the state of nature', I have in mind all the claims of moral right that would be intelligible outside the conventional institutional context of civil government.

7   John Rawls, 'Two Concepts of Rules', *Philosophical Review* (1955). Though Rawls's views are in many respects very Kantian, it is interesting and illuminating to see how they differ from Kant's in certain crucial respects. Very roughly, Rawls attempts to show that it would be immoral to adopt a practice or institution which would permit, as one of its rules, the 'punishment' of the innocent. But this rule is to be attacked, according to Rawls, on utilitarian grounds, i.e. by arguing that no one could feel secure or happy living under such an arbitrary or unjust system. Kant would, I think, agree that this is an important observation. However, he would want to oppose 'punishing' the innocent *on principle*, regardless of *any* utility. Thus Kant, unlike Rawls, is able to condemn as immoral even a private infliction of 'punishment' on an innocent man when it is known that such activities will not become extensive enough to be practices and thus pose a threat to everyone. Kant is not a utilitarian, even a sophisticated rule utilitarian. And it is important to keep this in mind, especially when considering Kant's retributive views on punishment. As H. L. A. Hart has observed, 'a theory of punishment which disregarded [retributive considerations] or viewed them simply as factors, frustration of which made for socially undesirable excitement, is a different kind of theory from one which *out of deference to those* [*considerations*] *themselves* restricts punishment...': *Punishment and Responsibility* (Oxford, 1968) p. 79 n.) In his later writings (e.g. 'Justice as Fairness'), Rawls has, I think, moved closer to the Kantian position.

8   Margaret Macdonald, 'Natural Rights', in *Philo-*

168

sophy, Politics and Society, First Series, ed. Peter Laslett (Oxford, 1963).

9   At paragraph 57, Locke *says* something quite similar. But his commitment to an extreme utilitarianism keeps him from appreciating the importance of what he has said. Like many utilitarians, he fails to see that freedom and the common good are *different* and often competing social values. Thus he can say in this same paragraph that an interference with freedom is not *really* an interference if it works for a good consequence. For 'that ill deserves the name of confinement which hedges us in only from bogs and precipices'.

10   I have changed Ladd's 'have his own right' (which is a correct translation from the German) to 'claim his own right' since it is clear that Kant is *denying* here that we really do have such a natural right. Indeed, at 237 (Ladd, 43) Kant claims that there is only one innate or natural right – freedom. See also 348 (Ladd, 121–2), where Kant argues that the notion of a punitive war, since it could rest on no principle of justice, is self-contradictory.

11   These procedural institutions will, of course, be administered by humans and will thus not guarantee justice infallibly. They will go a long way towards eliminating injustice, however, and represent the best that is possible for a human community.

12   The distinction between the rights that can be ascribed in a state of nature and those which can only be ascribed in civil society gives Kant his distinction between Private Law and Public Law. Private Law rests simply on the principle that human relations must be controlled by demands of justice. Public Law involves all those acquired rights which (like punishing) can exist only in a civil community. Private Law is ultimately secured by Public Law.

13   It is important to see that whether or not an action is wrong and whether or not it is excusable are different questions. To hurt my secretary's feelings by extreme rudeness is surely morally wrong. But I could be excused for doing this if I laboured under extreme strain at the time. (Suppose I had just learned that my child had an incurable illness.) To excuse me is to

recognise that my moral failure could have been avoided only by more self-restraint than would be fair to demand of me in such circumstances. To excuse me is *not* to defend the new moral truth that it is morally permissible to hurt people's feelings so long as you do so under pressure. This would mean that no wrong had been done to my secretary, and that is absurd.

14 In a famous English necessity case, Lord Coleridge, C.J., used a remarkably Kantian argument to support his belief that one is not justified in taking the life of another to save one's own: 'Who is to be the judge of this sort of necessity? By what measure is the comparative value of lives to be measured? Is it to be strength, or intellect, or what? It is plain that the principle leaves to him who is to profit by it to determine the necessity which will justify him in deliberately taking another's life to save his own.' Coleridge also regarded such action as not excusable (*R. v. Dudley and Stephens* (1884), 14 Q.B.D. 273).

15 Some conservative *laissez-faire* economists argue that such defects result from the impersonal mechanics of the market and not from voluntary human agency. Thus they are no more properly called injustices than are natural disasters like floods. But this is confused. Though in origin the market was not a product of human design, it is (unlike a flood) subject to correction or replacement by voluntary human intervention.

16 At *Justice*, 256 (Ladd, 66) Kant argues that the obligation to adopt a rule of law entails the right to compel others, even if they are not willing, to adopt it as well. But it is hard to see how this can be squared with Kant's view that coercion is justified only *within* a social practice. To say that the compulsion is justified for their own good would smack of just that kind of paternalism that Kant, as a defender of freedom, is supposed to oppose. To say that it is justified for the good of others would smack of just that kind of utilitarianism that Kant, as a defender of justice, is supposed to oppose. At *Justice*, 312 (Ladd, 76–7) Kant even toys with the Hobbesian notion that questions of justice are *meaningless* in a state of nature and thus no moral objection may be raised against the use of vio-

170

lent means to compel people to enter civil society. But this is clearly not Kant's considered view. If it were, he could hardly claim (as he repeatedly does) that there is a *moral obligation* to leave the state of nature.

17 Though Kant is quite right in insisting that moral judgments are not empirical claims, he often fails to notice that such claims are sometimes relevant in *support* of a moral judgment. Like most Enlightenment theorists, Kant is content to defend representative government by arguing that, *in theory*, it ought to maximise freedom. But he never considers the question of whether it does so *in fact*. And this question might yield some surprising answers. See, in this regard, C. B. Macpherson, 'The Maximisation of Democracy', in *Philosophy, Politics and Society, Third Series*, ed. Peter Laslett and W. G. Runciman (Oxford, 1967).

18 'The law of a reciprocal use of coercion that is necessarily consistent with everyone's freedom under the principle of universal freedom may in certain respects be regarded as the *construction* of the concept of justice' (*Justice*, 233; Ladd, 37). See also John Rawls, 'Legal Obligation and the Duty of Fair Play', in *Law and Philosophy*, ed. Sidney Hook (New York, 1964).

19 In spite of the bad press Kant has received for his views on revolution, he is not insensitive to the ways that violence can become institutionalised in government so as to repress its citizens. In a generally ignored note at *Justice*, 320–1 (Ladd, 87), Kant suggests that revolution, though always wrong, might be *excusable* in circumstances of extreme oppression. Kant suggests that 'the people might have at least some excuse for forcibly bringing this about by appealing to the right of necessity'.

20 One reason why Kant may have felt obliged to oppose all resistance to government was his belief that a government can have no legal limitations: 'The sovereign in the state has many rights with respect to the subject but no (coercive) duties' (*Justice*, 319; Ladd, 85). But this, like most sovereignty theory, is confused. Though a community might have some authority whose decisions are ultimately binding, it

does not follow from this that this authority does not have its own office and powers defined by legal rules. In America, for example, the Supreme Court has final authority over constitutional questions. It does not follow from this that the Constitution is just whatever the court says it is. For an elaboration of this point, see Hart, *The Concept of Law*, chap. iv.

21 There are two possible arguments that might be urged against even this limited form of resistance: (1) *The man who decides that his government is acting contrary to law is still acting as judge in his own case.* Of course, in this respect we all always act as judges in our own case. If we did not, moral action would not be possible; for we surely have to make decisions based on imperfect knowledge and imperfect objectivity. Kant's prohibition against being judge in one's own case is to hold only with respect to the use of *violence*. The dangerousness of error here is so great that extraordinary precautions are required. (2) *The man who even passively refuses to obey a law is a parasite; he is taking a liberty he could not extend to others.* The strength of this objection depends upon how we describe the agent's action. Opponents of civil disobedience will tend to characterise it as 'disobeying laws you don't like'; and, of course, the action is not universalisable on this characterisation. But is this the most plausible characterisation? If the action is, for example, described as 'disobedience to a law which one on reflection believes to be profoundly immoral', then it is by no means clear that it is non-universalisable. Another relevant point about conscientious disobedience is the following: Kant claims that it is unjust to bind a man to a law that he could not have assented to in an antecedent position of choice. But would a man, understanding what it is to hold a moral principle, contract away his right to base his decisions on that principle? A man may contract away a substantial portion of his prudential autonomy, but would a rational man contract away his moral autonomy?

22 The class of fanatical utilitarians is not as small as one might hope. Witness the agitation for 'sexual psychopath laws' and other procedures for the preventive

detention of those believed to be potentially dangerous to the community. Since the deprivation of liberty involved is called 'therapy' instead of 'punishment', it is easy to forget that substantial issues of freedom and due process are involved. For a probing discussion of the issues here, see Thomas S. Szsaz, *Law, Liberty and Psychiatry* (New York, 1963).

23 In his theory of punishment, Kant places certain limitations on his retributive belief that like should be returned for like. The State should never, Kant argues, do anything to a criminal that humiliates and degrades his dignity as a man. Though Kant's conception of reciprocity explains why the guilty should be punished, it is not clear that this same principle will explain Kant's belief that like should be returned for like, that the evil inflicted on the criminal should be of equal gravity with that which the criminal has inflicted on others (*jus talionis*). The criminal has acted unfairly, and that is why he must be punished. But unfairness is unfairness, murder being no more *unfair* than robbery. Thus if murder is worse than robbery (and thus deserves a worse punishment), this cannot be shown on the basis of purely formal or conceptual considerations. In his *Philosophy of Right*, Hegel (unlike Kant) distinguishes sharply the general principle of retribution from the principle of like for like, and argues (quite correctly in my judgment) that the argument to establish the general retributive principle will not be sufficient to determine, for all cases, the exact nature and manner of punishment. Consider, for example, the punishment for rape and abortion if the 'like for like' position were taken seriously. If it be argued that the position does not entail that we rape the rapist but only do to him something of *equal* evil, it can be replied that the question 'What evils *are* equal?' does not admit of a purely formal answer.

24 This very plausible analysis of what it can mean to say that a man wills his own punishment is ironic because it occurs in a passage where Kant is attempting to argue (in a discussion of Beccaria) that it makes *no sens*e to say that a man wills his own punishment. The wisdom, in my judgment, lies with the analysis.

Though men do not desire their punishment, they can be said rationally to will or consent to it in Kant's contractual sense.

25 The fact that taxation is such a minimal form of coercion is important to note. If we were talking about the massive coercive sanctions of the *criminal* law, then we would properly be much more cautious in enforcing the duty of helping others in distress. Since we all fail so drastically in matters of benevolence to others (paying our taxes for welfare is about all most of us do), we would all deserve to be punished for our omissions if helping others became a duty in the criminal law. Caution here can, of course, be carried to an extreme. As American law now stands, I would not be criminally responsible for failing to lift a drowning child's head out of the water – even if I could do this with no sacrifice to myself – unless the child was my legal charge. For a variety of discussions of the issues involved here, see *The Good Samaritan and the Law*, ed. James M. Ratcliffe (Garden City, 1966).

26 It should be noted that economic deprivation can make it impossible *in fact* (if not in theory) for those so deprived to exercise certain rights and enjoy certain governmental services, e.g. education, police protection, effective political participation. If Kant would want to grant even the poorest these rights (as he surely should), he should be worried that they lack the necessary conditions for exercising them. Otherwise his concern with freedom, and with all rights based on freedom, will seem insincere and hollow. Or to put the point another way: A rational man might surely contract into a society in which his happiness would not be positively promoted. But would he contract into a society which might let him suffer deprivation so extensive that he could exercise none of the rights formally promised by that society? This may be the point Kant is misleadingly expressing in the previously quoted passage.

Appendix

1 See Barry Stroud, 'Transcendental Arguments',

174

Journal of Philosophy (1968), and Stephan Körner, 'The Impossibility of Transcendental Deductions', *The Monist* (1967).

2   Two recent issues of *The Monist* (July and October 1967) were devoted to the topic 'Kant Today'. The essays included demonstrate the contemporary interest in and inuence of Kant's philosophy. These essays, along with several others, have been published as the volume *Kant Studies Today*, ed. Lewis White Beck (La Salle, 1969).

Select Bibliography

The following bibliography makes no pretence of being complete. It is rather a list of recommended further readings (in English) that are likely to be available in a university library. The emphasis is on the moral-political philosophy, and some of the listings, though not specifically on Kant, are included because they pursue Kantian themes in an interesting way. For a much fuller listing of secondary material, consult M. J. Scott-Taggart, 'Recent Work on the Philosophy of Kant', *American Philosophical Quarterly* (1966). An updated reprinting of this article may be found in *Kant Studies Today*, ed. Lewis White Beck (La Salle, 1969).

Works by Kant

Critique of Pure Reason (1st and 2nd eds), trans. Norman Kemp Smith (London, 1933).

Prolegomena to Any Future Metaphysics, trans. Lewis White Beck (Indianapolis, 1950).

Kant's Inaugural Dissertation, trans. John Handyside (Chicago, 1929).

Lectures on Ethics, trans. Louis Infield (New York, 1963).

Foundations of the Metaphysics of Morals, trans. Lewis White Beck (Indianapolis, 1959).

Critique of Practical Reason, trans. Lewis White Beck (Indianapolis, 1956).

Critique of Judgment, trans. James Creed Meredith (Oxford, 1952).

Religion Within the Limits of Reason Alone, trans. T. M. Greene and Hoyt H. Hudson (New York, 1960).

Concerning the Common Saying: This May be True in Theory but does not Apply in Practice, trans. Carl

176

J. Friedrich, in his Kant anthology *The Philosophy of Kant* (New York, 1949).

Perpetual Peace, trans. Lewis White Beck, in his Kant anthology *On History* (Indianapolis, 1963).

The Metaphysical Elements of Justice (Pt. i, *Rechtslehre*, of the *Metaphysics of Morals*), trans. John Ladd (Indianapolis, 1965). This is not a complete translation.

The Doctrine of Virtue (Pt. ii, *Tungendlehre*, of the *Metaphysics of Morals*), trans. Mary J. Gregor (New York, 1964).

The *Tugendlehre* has also been well translated, as *The Metaphysical Principles of Virtue*, by James Ellington (Indianapolis, 1964).

The Ladd, Gregor and Ellington translations all contain the Introduction to the *Metaphysics of Morals* as a whole.

Commentaries

Lewis White Beck, *A Commentary on Kant's Critique of Practical Reason* (Chicago, 1960). It would be hard to overestimate the excellence of this commentary. It is both scholarly and philosophically interesting, and these qualities rarely go together in Kant studies.

——, *Studies in the Philosophy of Kant* (Indianapolis, 1965). This is a collection of Beck's important articles. Most relevant to the present study are 'Kant's Theoretical and Practical Philosophy', 'Sir David Ross on Duty and Purpose in Kant', 'Apodictic Imperatives' and 'Kant's Two Conceptions of the Will in Their Political Context'.

Jonathan Bennett, *Kant's Analytic* (Cambridge, 1966). This is a very philosophically stimulating book on Kant's first *Critique*. The connection of the argument with Kant's text, however, is sometimes difficult to trace.

Mary J. Gregor, *Laws of Freedom* (Oxford, 1963). In some ways this is a disturbingly cautious book, but it is a solid study that is surely the best work in English on Kant's material moral philosophy. Her emphasis in the book is on Kant's theory of virtue rather than his theory of right.

John Kemp, *The Philosophy of Kant* (London, 1968). One can never be very happy with a short survey of Kant's thought (including that by the present author), but Kemp's little book provides a sound general introduction. For the beginner student it would make a useful supplement to the present work in that it is (i) more traditional and scholarly in its approach to Kant's epistemology and metaphysics and (ii) not directed toward the issues of social and political ethics.

H. J. Paton, *The Categorical Imperative* (London, 1947). This is a fine book that represented, in many ways, a breakthrough in the interpretation of Kant's ethics. Its major weakness is a kind of pious devotion to Kant that prevents the author from being as critical as one would like. Much the same can be said for the same author's *Kant's Metaphysic of Experience*, 2 vols (London, 1936), a commentary on Kant's first *Critique*.

Norman Kemp Smith, *A Commentary to Kant's 'Critique of Pure Reason'*, 2nd ed. (London, 1923). This is an excellent commentary on Kant's first *Critique*, careful but much more critical than, say, Paton. It is for dipping into, not for reading straight through.

P. F. Strawson, *The Bounds of Sense* (London, 1966). In my judgment this is a masterpiece – the best commentary on Kant's first *Critique* ever written. It is like Bennett's in that it attempts to discuss Kant in a contemporary idiom, but it is much more closely tied to the text.

T. D. Weldon, *Kant's Critique of Pure Reason*, 2nd ed. (Oxford, 1958). Many scholars prefer the first edition of this work because they feel it is less 'cluttered up' with points drawn from 'linguistic philosophy'. Rather timidly, I must confess to finding the second edition much more interesting.

Robert Paul Wolff, *Kant's Theory of Mental Activity* (Cambridge, Mass., 1963). This is a commentary on the Transcendental Analytic of the first *Critique*, somewhat in the manner of Weldon. It is very informative and gives the reader the strong sense that
178

an *argument* is being developed. Too many Kant commentaries read like strings of unconnected observations tied together with some unintelligible quotes, and Wolff's is a refreshing change from that sort of thing. Wolff has also edited a useful collection of essays: *Kant* (Garden City, 1967).

Relevant Books and Articles

This is primarily a list of useful articles, but I have included a few books that could hardly be called 'commentaries' on Kant. The journal *Kant-Studien*, which publishes some articles in English, would merit the student's perusal.

A. C. Armstrong, 'Kant's Philosophy of Peace and War', *Journal of Philosophy* (1931).

Lewis White Beck, *Studies in the Philosophy of Kant*, noted above.

S. I. Benn and R. S. Peters, *The Principles of Political Thought* (New York, 1959). This is an excellent analytical introduction to political and legal philosophy. It was originally published in England under the title *Social Principles and the Democratic State* (London 1959).

John Bourke, 'Kant's Doctrine of "Perpetual Peace"', *Philosophy* (1942).

Stuart M. Brown Jr., 'Has Kant a Philosophy of Law?', *Philosophical Review* (1961).

Paul Dietrichson, 'When is a Maxim Fully Universalisable?', *Kant-Studien* (1964).

Carl J. Friedrich, *Inevitable Peace* (Cambridge, Mass., 1948).

Alan Gewirth, 'Categorial Consistency in Ethics', *Philosophical Quarterly* (1967).

Pepita Haezrahi, 'The Concept of Man as End-in-Himself', *Kant-Studien* (1962).

Robert W. Hall, 'Kant and Ethical Formalism', *Kant-Studien* (1960–1).

R. N. Hancock, 'Kant and the Natural Right Theory', *Kant-Studien* (1960–1).

R. M. Hare, 'Universalisability', *Proceedings of the*

Aristotelian Society (1954–5).

Jonathan Harrison, 'Kant's Examples of the First Formulation of the Categorical Imperative', *Philosophical Quarterly* (1957). John Kemp replied to this article in his 'Kant's Examples of the Categorical Imperative' (1958), and Harrison published 'The Categorical Imperative' (1958) as a rejoinder.

H. L. A. Hart, *The Concept of Law* (Oxford, 1961). This is probably the best book in legal philosophy ever written, and it could be profitably read by a student as an introduction to the subject.

——, 'Are There Any Natural Rights?', *The Philosophical Review* (1955).

F. A. von Hayek, 'The Principles of a Liberal Social Order', in his *Studies in Philosophy, Politics and Economics* (Chicago, 1967).

John Ladd, 'Kant's View on the Relation of Law to Morality', *Journal of Philosophy* (1960).

——, Introduction, in Kant, *The Metaphysical Elements of Justice*, trans. by John Ladd (Indianapolis 1965).

David Lyons, *Forms and Limits of Utilitarianism* (Oxford, 1965). This is one of the best critical studies of utilitarianism ever written.

W. I. Matson, 'Kant as Casuist', *Journal of Philosophy* (1954).

Donald Meiklejohn, 'Kantian Formalism and Civil Liberty', *Journal of Philosophy* (1954).

Herbert Morris, 'Punishment for 'Thoughts', *The Monist* (1965).

——, 'Persons and Punishment', *The Monist* (1968). Though Kant is not explicitly discussed in these articles, Morris pursues the topic of punishment in an illuminating and very Kantian way.

Jeffrie G. Murphy, 'The Highest Good as Content for Kant's Ethical Formalism', *Kant-Studien* (1965). This is a critical discussion of some of John Silber's work.

——, 'Kant's Concept of a Right Action', *The Monist* (1967). Reprinted in *Kant Studies Today*, ed. Lewis White Beck (La Salle, 1968).

——, 'A Paradox in Locke's Theory of Natural Rights', *Dialogue* (1969).
180

Jeffrie G. Murphy, 'Violence and the Rule of Law', forthcoming in *Ethics*.

——, 'Kant's Theory of Criminal Punishment', forthcoming in *The Proceedings of the Third International Kant Congress*.

Jan Narveson, 'Pacifism: A Philosophical Analysis', *Ethics* (1965). This is an argument that a position of total pacifism is self-contradictory. It is very like Kant's argument for the moral title.

H. J. Paton, 'An Alleged Right to Lie: A Problem in Kantian Ethics', *Kant-Studien* (1953–4).

John Rawls, 'Justice as Fairness', *Philosophical Review* (1958). This article has been reprinted in *Philosophy, Politics and Society, Second Series*, Peter Laslett and W. G. Runciman (Oxford, 1964).

——, 'Legal Obligation and the Duty of Fair Play', in *Law and Philosophy*, ed. Sidney Hook (New York, 1964).

——, 'Constitutional Liberty and the Concept of Justice', in *Nomos VI: Justice*, ed. Carl J. Friedrich and John W. Chapman (New York, 1963),

H. S. Reiss, 'Kant and the Right to Rebellion', *Journal of the History of Ideas* (1956).

Gilbert Ryle, 'Categories', *Proceedings of the Aristotelian Society* (1937–8).

Wolfgang Schwarz, 'Kant's Philosophy of Law and International Peace', *Philosophy and Phenomenological Research* (1962).

John R. Silber, 'The Context of Kant's Ethical Thought', *Philosophical Quarterly* (1959).

——, 'The Copernican Revolution in Ethics: The Good Re-examined', *Kant-Studien* (1959–60).

——, 'Kant's Conception of the Highest Good as Immanent and Transcendent', *Philosophical Review* (1959).

——, 'The Importance of the Highest Good in Kant's Ethics', *Ethics* (1962–3).

The doctrine of the *summum bonum* is important in Kant's ethics, but it has been beside my purpose to discuss it in the present work. Silber's articles are a fine introduction to the topic.

Marcus Singer, 'The Categorical Imperative', *Philo-*
181

sophical Review (1954). This forms a part of his *Generalization in Ethics* (New York, 1961).

W. H. Walsh, 'Categories', *Kant-Studien* (1953–4).

Warner Wick, Introduction ('Kant's Moral Philosophy'), in Kant, *The Metaphysical Principles of Virtue*, trans. James Ellington (Indianapolis, 1964).

Name Index

Subject Index